Samuel Beckett
A Checklist of Criticism

Samuel Beckett

A Checklist of Criticism

By James T. F. Tanner and J. Don Vann

The Kent State University Press

The Serif Series:
Bibliographies and Checklists, / Number 8

William White, General Editor
Wayne State University

SBN 87338-051-7
Library of Congress Card Catalogue Number 70-626232
Manufactured in the United States of America
at the press of The Oberlin Printing Company
Designed by Merald E. Wrolstad

First Edition

Introduction

Although Samuel Beckett published his first book-length work
as early as 1930, he did not attract widespread critical and
scholarly attention until the 1950's and 60's; the first critical
volume devoted to him did not appear until 1957, and the first
extensive critical study in English not until the year 1962.
Thus, interest in Samuel Beckett's work is a phenomenon
peculiar to the present decade and that immediately preceding
it. Such critical and scholarly interest shows no signs of abating.
This will be evident to anyone who thumbs through our present
compilation. It is designed to encourage and facilitate critical
and scholarly study of Samuel Beckett's works.

Our intention has been simply to provide a checklist of
criticism *about* Samuel Beckett. We have not interested ourselves
in Beckett's primary works, except that at the close of this
introduction we list, for the convenience of the researcher,
Beckett's major books in chronological order.

We believe our arrangement of materials will be especially
helpful to the student seeking information on specific aspects
of Beckett's work. Separate sections devoted to bibliographies,
books about Beckett, chapters about Beckett in books,
articles about Beckett, and reviews of Beckett's books are
designed to send the researcher quickly and painlessly to his goal.
In the section on books about Beckett, we provide a selective
list of reviews of such books; quite often the researcher

wishes to know exactly in what esteem a particular book is held by the author's peers.

We have made this compilation as complete as possible, but we are not foolish enough to suppose that it is exhaustive. Because of Beckett's linguistic versatility, the fact that he writes in practically all genres, the widespread interest in his work, the numerous individuals everywhere who write about him in obscure as well as established journalistic outlets—because of all these facts, we know that this bibliography is only reasonably complete. It is, we feel, lengthy enough to allow the construction from it of various briefer bibliographies (as, for example, "Beckett and Existentialism," or "Beckett and the Theatre of the Absurd," *et cetera*) which should facilitate study of all aspects of Beckett's art.

We must acknowledge our indebtedness to previous bibliographers whose names appear below in the section on bibliographies. Our colleague, Professor James Lee, who did some early work on this bibliography, was kind enough to make available to us the results of his work. We are grateful to the Committee on Faculty Research of North Texas State University for allowing us released time from teaching and for providing clerical assistance. Our general editor, Professor William White of Wayne State University, has been especially helpful in the preparation of this manuscript. Finally, we appreciate the unstinting labor of our two research assistants, Miss Susan Hartley and Mr. Richard Kelch.

JAMES T. F. TANNER
J. DON VANN

Denton, Texas

Beckett's Major Books
A Chronological Listing

Whoroscope. Paris: Hours Press, 1930.

Proust. London: Chatto and Windus, 1931. Reprinted, New York: Grove Press, 1957.

More Pricks than Kicks. London: Chatto and Windus, 1934.

Echo's Bones. Paris: Europa Press, 1935.

Murphy. London: Routledge, 1938. Reprinted, New York: Grove Press, 1957.

Murphy. Translated into French by the author. Paris: Bordas, 1947.

Molloy. Paris: Edition de Minuit, 1951.

Malone Meurt. Paris: Edition de Minuit, 1952.

En Attendant Godot. Paris: Edition de Minuit, 1952.

L'Innommable. Paris: Edition de Minuit, 1953.

Watt. Paris: Olympia Press, 1953.

Waiting for Godot. New York: Grove Press, 1954.

Molloy. New York: Grove Press, 1955.

Nouvelles et Textes pour rien. Paris: Edition de Minuit, 1955.

1

All that Fall. London: Faber & Faber; New York: Grove Press, 1957.

Fin de Partie suivi de Acte sans Paroles. Paris: Edition de Minuit, 1957.

From an Abandoned Work. London: Faber & Faber, 1957.

Tous ceux qui tombent. Paris: Edition de Minuit, 1957.

Anthology of Mexican Poetry. Translated by Samuel Beckett. Compiled by Octavio Paz. Bloomington: University of Indiana Press; London: Thames & Hudson, 1958.

Endgame followed by Act Without Words. New York: Grove Press, 1958.

Malone Dies. New York: Grove Press, 1956; London: Calder, 1958.

The Unnamable. New York: Grove Press, 1958.

Watt. London: Zwemmer, 1958; New York: Grove Press, 1959.

La dernière bande. Traduit de l'anglais par Pierre Leyris et l'auteur. Suivi de *Cendres* pièce radiophonique. Paris: Edition de Minuit, 1959.

Gedichte. Wiesbaden: Limes, 1959.

Henri Hayden. London: The Waddington Galleries, 1959.

Krapp's Last Tape and Embers. London: Faber & Faber, 1959.

Trilogy: Molloy; Malone Dies; and The Unnamable. New York: Grove Press; London: Calder, 1959.

Bram von Velde. New York: Grove Press, 1960.

Krapp's Last Tape and Other Dramatic Pieces. New York: Grove Press, 1960. [Contains *Krapp's Last Tape, All that Fall, Embers, Act Without Words I, Act Without Words II.*]

Comment c'est. Paris: Edition de Minuit, 1961.

Happy Days. New York: Grove Press, 1961.

Poems in English. London: Calder, 1961; New York: Grove Press, 1962.

Dramatische Dichtungen. Französiche Originalfassungen. Deutsch Ubertragen von Elmer Tophoven. Englische Ubertragung von Samuel Beckett. Frankfurt: Suhrkamp, 1963.

Oh, les beaux jours. Paris: Edition de Minuit, 1963.

How It Is. London: Calder; New York: Grove Press, 1964.

Play, and Two Short Pieces for the Radio. London: Faber & Faber, 1964.

Imagination morte imaginez. Paris: Edition de Minuit, 1965.

Assez. Paris: Edition de Minuit, 1966.

Bing! Paris: Edition de Minuit, 1966.

Comédie et actes divers. Paris: Edition de Minuit, 1966.

Imagination Dead Imagine. London: Calder & Boyars, 1966.

Come and Go: Dramaticule. London: Calder & Boyars, 1967.

Eh Joe and Other Writings. London: Faber & Faber, 1967.

No's Knife: *Collected Shorter Prose, 1945-1966.* London: Calder & Boyars, 1967.

A Samuel Beckett Reader. Edited by John Calder. London: Calder & Boyars, 1967.

Stories and Texts for Nothing. New York: Grove Press, 1967.

Têtes-mortes. Paris: Edition de Minuit, 1967.

A. Bibliographies

Bryer, J. R. "Critique de Samuel Beckett: Sélection bibliographique." *La Revue des lettres modernes*, No. 100 (1964), pp. 169-184.

Cohn, Ruby. "A Checklist of Beckett Criticism," *Perspective*, XI (Autumn 1959), 193-196.

―――. "A Checklist . . ." *Casebook on Waiting for Godot, The Impact of Beckett's Modern Classic: Reviews, Reflections, and Interpretations.* New York: Grove Press, 1967, pp. 188-192.

―――. *Samuel Beckett: The Comic Gamut.* New Brunswick: Rutgers University Press, 1962, pp. 328-338.

Esslin, Martin. *The Theatre of the Absurd.* New York: Doubleday, 1961, pp. 317-319.

Fletcher, John. *The Novels of Samuel Beckett.* New York: Barnes & Noble, 1964, pp. 234-251.

Hoffman, Frederick J. *Samuel Beckett: The Language of Self.* Carbondale: Southern Illinois University Press, 1962, pp. 170-172.

Jacobsen, Josephine, and William R. Mueller. *The Testament of Samuel Beckett: A Study.* New York: Hill and Wang, 1964, pp. 175, 177-178.

B. Books About Beckett

Calder, John, ed. *Beckett at Sixty*: *A Festschrift.* London: Calder, 1967.

REVIEWS

Burgess, Anthony. *Spectator*, CCXIX (21 July 1967), 79.
Hodgart, Matthew. *Manchester Guardian*, XCVII (27 July 1967), 11.
Johnson, Bryan S. *New Statesman*, LXXIV (14 July 1967), 54.
Kingston, J. *Punch*, CCLIII (2 August 1967), 182.
Ricks, Christopher. *Listener*, LXXVIII (3 August 1967), 148.
Wilson, A. *Observer* (London), 16 July 1967, p. 20.

Coe, Richard N. *Samuel Beckett.* New York: Grove Press; Edinburgh: Oliver, 1964.

REVIEWS

Davison, P. *Modern Language Review*, LX (1965), 610-612.
Whittington-Egan, R. *Books & Bookmen*, X (January 1965), 34.
Unsigned. *Choice*, II (October 1965), 488.
———. *Times Literary Supplement* (London), 17 December 1964, p. 1146.

Cohn, Ruby. *Samuel Beckett: The Comic Gamut*. New
Brunswick: Rutgers University Press, 1962.

REVIEWS

Friedman, Melvin J. *Comparative Literature*, xvi (1964),
264-269.

Griffin, Lloyd W. *Library Journal*, 6 October 1962, p. 43.

Guerard, Albert J. *Saturday Review*, 6 October 1962,
pp. 51-52.

Hesla, David H. *Critique*, vi (Fall 1963), 103-108.

Unsigned. *Times Literary Supplement* (London),
21 December 1962, p. 988.

————, ed. *Casebook on Waiting for Godot; The Impact
of Beckett's Modern Classic: Reviews, Reflections,
and Interpretations*. New York: Grove Press, 1967.

REVIEW

McAneny, M. *Library Journal*, xcii (1 December 1967),
4417.

Delye, Huguette. *Samuel Beckett ou la philosophie de l'absurde*.
Aix en Provence: la pensée universitaire, 1960.

Esslin, Martin, ed. *Samuel Beckett: A Collection of Critical
Essays*. Englewood Cliffs: Prentice-Hall, 1965.

REVIEWS

Cohn, Ruby. *Southern Review* (Summer 1966), p. 714.

Driver, Tom F. *New York Times Book Review*,
23 January 1966, p. 4.

Karl, Frederick R. *Western Humanities Review* (Autumn
1966), p. 362.

Unsigned. *Choice*, iii (March 1966), 36.

————. *Christian Century*, LXXXII (8 December 1965),
1515.

————. *Library Journal*, XCI (15 February 1966), 1082.

————. *New York Times Book Review*, 23 January 1966,
p. 4.

Federman, Raymond. *Journey to Chaos*: *Samuel Beckett's
Early Fiction*. Berkeley: University of California Press,
1965. London: Cambridge University Press.

REVIEWS

Cohn, Ruby. *Southern Review* (Summer 1966), p. 714.

Driver, Tom F. *New York Times Book Review*, 23 January
1966, p. 4.

Strauss, Walter A. *Modern Language Journal*, L
(November 1966), 505.

Unsigned. *Choice*, II (January 1966), 776.

————. *New York Times Book Review*, 23 January 1966,
p. 4.

————. *Times Literary Supplement* (London), 5 May
1966, p. 388.

Fletcher, John. *The Novels of Samuel Beckett*. London:
Chatto and Windus, 1964.

REVIEWS

Bates, R. *Canadian Forum*, XLV (August 1965), 118.

Cruikshank, John. *Durham University Journal*, n.s.,
XXVII (1965), 498.

Donoghue, Denis. *New Statesman*, LXVIII (1964), 498.

Gurko, Leo. *English Language Notes* (March 1965),
p. 242.

Johnson, Bryan S. *Spectator*, CCXIII (28 August 1964), 280.

Unsigned. *Times Literary Supplement* (London),
3 September 1964, p. 808.

———. *Samuel Beckett's Art*. New York: Barnes and Noble, 1967.

REVIEWS

Sprague, Claire. *New York Times Book Review*, 12 November 1967, p. 67.
Unsigned. *Choice*, IV (October 1967), 842.

———. *Technique et Méthodes littéraires dans l'oeuvre de Samuel Beckett*. Thèse dactylographiée, Toulouse, 1965.

Gessner, Niklaus. *Die Unzulänglichkeit der Sprache. Eine Untersuchung über formzerfall und Beziehungslosigkeit bei Samuel Beckett*. Zürich: Juris Verlag, 1957.

Hassan, Ihab H. *The Literature of Silence*: *Henry Miller and Samuel Beckett*. New York: Knopf, 1968.

Hoffman, Frederick J. *Samuel Beckett*: *The Language of Self*. Carbondale: Southern Illinois University Press, 1962.

REVIEWS

Butcher, Fanny. *Chicago Sunday Tribune*, 4 March 1962, p. 6.
Griffin, Lloyd W. *Library Journal*, LXXXVII (15 May 1962), 1905.
Hesla, David H. *Critique*, VI (Fall 1963), 103-108.
Hicks, Granville. *Saturday Review*, XLV (23 June 1962), 26.
Unsigned. *Times Literary Supplement* (London), 21 December 1962, p. 988.

Jacobsen, Josephine, and William R. Mueller. *The Testament of Samuel Beckett*: *A Study*. New York: Hill and Wang, 1964; London: Faber, 1966.

REVIEWS

Hesla, David H. *Christian Scholar*, XLVIII (1965), 318-320.

Pryce, Jones A. *New York Herald Tribune*, 29 February 1964, p. 13.

Segesta, J. *Library Journal*, LXXXIX (15 February 1964), 868.

Smalley, W. *Quarterly Journal of Speech*, LI (February 1965), 96.

Sutherland, D. *New Leader*, 11 May 1964, p. 12.

Janvier, Ludovic. *Pour Samuel Beckett*. Paris: Editions de Minuit, 1966.

Kenner, Hugh. *Flaubert, Joyce, and Beckett: The Stoic Comedians*. London: W. H. Allen, 1964.

REVIEWS

Goldgar, Harry. *Comparative Literature*, XV (1964), 371-373.

Pallette, D. B. *Arizona Quarterly*, XX (1964), 88-89.

Porteous, Hugh Gordon. *Spectator*, CCXII (3 April 1964), 455.

Weeks, Donald. *Journal of Aesthetics and Art Criticism*, XXII (1963), 226-227.

Unsigned. *Times Literary Supplement* (London), 16 April 1964, p. 313.

————. *Samuel Beckett: A Critical Study*. New York: Grove Press, 1962.

REVIEWS

Davenport, Guy. *National Review*, XII (8 May 1962), 330-332.

Davie, Donald. *Manchester Guardian*, 26 October 1962,
   p. 6.
Esslin, Martin. *Listener*, LXVIII (1962), 923.
Hesla, David H. *Critique*, VI (Fall 1963), 103-108.
Johnson, Bryan S. *Spectator*, CCIX (23 November 1962),
   816, 818.
Kermode, Frank. *New Statesman*, LXIV (1962), 622.
Lid, Richard W. *San Francisco Sunday Chronicle*, 27 May
   1962, p. 31. [*This World.*]
Rogers, W. G. *Saturday Review*, 17 February 1962, p. 31.
Spender, Stephen. *New York Times Book Review*,
   25 February 1962, pp. 7, 32.
Vámosi, Pál. *Helikon*, XI (1965), 131-132.
Unsigned. *The Times* (London), 8 November 1962, p. 15.
————. *Times Literary Supplement* (London), 21
   December 1962, p. 988.

Maerli, Terje. *Samuel Beckett*. Oslo: Universitetsforlaget, 1967.

Melèse, Pierre. *Beckett*. Paris: Seghers, 1966.

Mueller, William R. See Jacobsen, Josephine.

Schoell, Konrad. *Das Theater Samuel Becketts*. Freiburger
   Schriften zur romanischen Philologie 11. München:
   Wilhelm Fink, 1967.

Scott, Nathan A., Jr. *Samuel Beckett*. London: Bowes; Toronto:
   Queenswood; New York: Hillary House, 1965.

   REVIEWS
   Davison, P. *Modern Language Review*, LX (1965),
      610-612.
   Harrison, K. *Spectator*, CCXIV (26 February 1965), 273.

Miller, S. H. *Journal of Religion*, XLVI (April 1966), 319.
Tindall, William York. *Romanic Review*, LVI (1965), 318.
Woodcock, George. *New Leader*, 7 June 1965, pp. 23-24.
Unsigned. *Times Literary Supplement* (London),
    25 March 1965, p. 236.

Simpson, Alan. *Beckett and Behan and a Theatre in Dublin*.
London: Routledge, 1962.

REVIEW

Federman, Raymond. *Modern Drama*, VIII (1965),
    123-124.

Tindall, William York. *Samuel Beckett*. New York; London:
Columbia University Press, 1964.

REVIEWS

Davison, P. *Modern Language Review*, LX (1965),
    610-612.
Harrison, K. *Spectator*, CCXIV (26 February 1965), 273.

C. Chapters About Beckett and References to Beckett in Books

Abel, Lionel. "Beckett and Metatheatre." In *Metatheatre.* New York: Hill and Wang, 1963, pp. 83-85.

———. "Samuel Beckett and James Joyce in *Endgame.*" In *Metatheatre.* New York: Hill and Wang, 1963, pp. 134-140.

Abirached, Robert. "Samuel Beckett." In *Écrivains d'au-jourd'hui, 1940-1960,* edited by Bernard Pingaud. Paris: B. Gresset, 1960, pp. 93-98.

Allsop, Kenneth. *The Angry Decade.* New York: British Book Centre, 1958, pp. 37-40.

Anders, Gunther. "Sein Ohne Zeit zu Becketts Stück *En attendant Godot.*" In *Die Antiquiertheit des Menschen Uber die Seele in Zeitalter de zweiten industriellen Revolution.* München: C. H. Beck, 1956, pp. 213-231.

Bentley, Eric. *The Life of the Drama.* New York: Atheneum, 1964, pp. 99-101, 348-351.

————. *What Is Theatre?* Boston: Beacon Press, 1956, *passim.*

Blanchot, Maurice. "Where Now? Who Now?" In *On Contemporary Literature*, edited by Richard Kostelanetz. New York: Avon Books, 1964, pp. 249-254.

Blau, Herbert. "Notes from the Underground," *The Impossible Theater*. New York: Macmillan, 1964. Reprinted in *Casebook on Waiting for Godot*, edited by Ruby Cohn. New York: Grove Press, 1967, pp. 113-121.

Block, Haskell M., and Robert G. Shedd. "Samuel Beckett (1906—)." In *Masters of Modern Drama*. New York: Random House, 1962, pp. 1102-1103.

Boisdeffre, Pierre de. "L'Anti-théâtre total: Beckett ou la mort de l'homme." *Une histoire vivante de la littérature d'aujourd'hui, 1938-1958*. Paris: Le Livre contemporaine, 1958, pp. 678-680.

————. "Samuel Beckett ou l'au-delà." *Une histoire vivante de la littérature d'aujourd'hui*. Paris: Le Livre contemporaine, 1957, pp. 299-300.

Brustein, Robert S. "Déjà vu." *Seasons of Discontent*. New York: Simon and Schuster, 1965, pp. 53-56.

————. "Listening to the Past." *Seasons of Discontent*. New York: Simon and Schuster, 1965, pp. 26-29.

Bull, Peter. "Peter Bull as Pozzo." *I Know the Face, But . . .* London: Peter Davies Ltd., 1959. Reprinted in *Casebook on Waiting for Godot*, edited by Ruby Cohn. New York: Grove Press, 1967, pp. 39-43.

Capone, Giovanna. *Drammi per voci: Dylan Thomas, Samuel Beckett, Harold Pinter*. Bologna: Patron, 1967.

Chiari, Joseph. *The Contemporary French Theatre—The Flight from Naturalism.* London: Rockliff, 1958, p. 226.

―――. *Landmarks of Contemporary Drama.* London: Herbert Jenkins, 1965, pp. 68-80.

Clurman, Harold. *"Happy Days."* In *The Naked Image: Observations on the Modern Theater.* New York: Macmillan, 1966, pp. 40-42.

―――. "Introduction." *Seven Plays of the Modern Theatre.* New York: Grove Press, 1962, pp. vii-xii.

―――. *Lies Like Truth.* New York: Macmillan, 1958, pp. 220-222.

―――. "The Lover and Beckett's *Play." The Naked Image: Observations on the Modern Theater.* New York: Macmillan, 1966, pp. 112-114.

―――. *"The Zoo Story* and Beckett's *Krapp's Last Tape." The Naked Image: Observations on the Modern Theater.* New York: Macmillan, 1966, pp. 13-15.

Ellmann, Richard. *James Joyce.* New York: Oxford University Press, 1959, *passim.*

Esslin, Martin. "Godot at San Quentin." *The Theatre of the Absurd.* New York: Doubleday and Company, 1961. Reprinted in *Casebook on Waiting for Godot,* edited by Ruby Cohn. New York: Grove Press, 1967, pp. 83-85.

―――. "Samuel Beckett." In *The Novelist as Philosopher,* edited by John Cruikshank. New York: Oxford University Press, 1962, pp. 128-146.

————. "Samuel Beckett: The Search for the Self." *The Theatre of the Absurd*. Garden City: Doubleday, 1961, pp. 1-46.

Federman, Raymond. "Beckett and the Fiction of Mud." In *On Contemporary Literature*, edited by Richard Kostelanetz. New York: Avon, 1964, pp. 255-261.

Fowlie, Wallace. "Beckett." *Dionysus in Paris*. New York: Meridian, 1960, pp. 210-217.

Fraser, G. S. See "Articles about Beckett" and "Reviews of Beckett's Books."

Gascoigne, Bamber. *Twentieth Century Drama*. London: Hutchinson, 1962, pp. 184-188.

Gassner, John. "European Vistas: Beckett's *Endgame* and Symbolism." *Theatre at the Crossroads*. New York: Holt, 1960, pp. 256-261.

————. "European Vistas: Beckett's *Waiting for Godot*." *Theatre at the Crossroads*. New York: Holt, 1960, pp. 252-256.

————. "They Also Serve." *Directions in Modern Theatre and Drama*: *An Expanded Edition of Form and Idea in Modern Theatre*. New York: Holt, 1965, pp. 318-323. [About *Waiting for Godot*.]

Glicksberg, Charles. *The Self in Modern Literature*. University Park, Pa.: Pennsylvania State University Press, 1963, pp. 117-121.

Goth, Maja. *Franz Kafka et les lettres françaises (1928-1955)*. Paris: José Corti, 1956, pp. 120-122.

Grossvogel, David I. *Four Playwrights and a Postscript.* Ithaca: Cornell University Press, 1962, pp. 85-131.

———. "Ionesco, Adamov, Beckett." *Self-Conscious Stage in Modern French Drama.* New York: Columbia University Press, 1958, pp. 324-334.

———. "Samuel Beckett: The Difficulty of Dying." *The Blasphemers: The Theatre of Brecht, Ionesco, Beckett, Genêt.* Ithaca: Cornell University Press, 1965, pp. 85-131.

Guicharnaud, Jacques. "Existence on Stage." In *On Contemporary Literature,* edited by Richard Kostelanetz. New York: Avon Books, 1964, pp. 262-285.

———. "Existence on Stage: Samuel Beckett." *Modern French Theatre from Girardoux to Beckett.* New Haven: Yale University Press, 1961, pp. 193-220.

Guiton, Margaret, and Germaine Brée. *An Age of Fiction.* New Brunswick, N. J.: Rutgers University Press, 1957, pp. 236-237.

Guggenheim, Marguerite. *Confessions of an Art Addict.* London: André Deutsch, 1960, p. 49.

Harwood, Timothy Blake. "Reid, A. Ireland." *Contemporary Patterns in European Writing.* Chester Springs, Pa.: Dufour Editions, 1966, pp. 38-43. [About *Krapp's Last Tape.*]

Hayman, David. "Quest for Meaninglessness: The Boundless Poverty of *Molloy.*" In *Six Contemporary Novels,* edited by W. O. S. Sutherland, Jr. Austin: University of Texas, 1962, pp. 90-112.

Heppenstall, Reyner. *The Fourfold Tradition*. London: Barrie and Rockliff, 1961; Norfolk, Conn.: New Directions, 1961, pp. 254-265.

Jacobsen, Josephine, and William R. Mueller. "Beckett's Long Saturday: To Wait or Not to Wait." In *Man in the Modern Theatre*, edited by Nathan A. Scott. Richmond, Va.: Knox, 1965, pp. 76-97.

Janvier, Ludovic. "Cyclical Dramaturgy." In *Pour Samuel Beckett*, edited by Ludovic Janvier. Paris: Les Editions de Minuit, 1966. Reprinted in *Casebook on Waiting for Godot*, edited by Ruby Cohn. New York: Grove Press, 1967, pp. 166-171.

Joyce, James. *Letters*. London: Faber & Faber, 1957. See index.

Karl, Frederick. "Waiting for Beckett: Quest and Re-Quest." *The Contemporary English Novel*. New York: Noonday Press, 1962, pp. 19-39.

Kenner, Hugh. "Samuel Beckett: Comedian of the Impasse." *Flaubert, Joyce, and Beckett: The Stoic Comedians*. London: W. H. Allen, 1964, pp. 67-107.

Kermode, Frank. "Beckett, Snow, and Pure Poverty." *Puzzles and Epiphanies: Essays and Reviews, 1958-1961*. New York: Chilmark Press, 1963, pp. 155-163.

Kesting, Marianne. *Das epische Theater: Zur Struktur des modernen Dramas*. Stuttgart: W. Kohlhammer, 1959.

Killinger, John. *The Failure of Theology in Modern Literature*. New York: Abingdon Press, 1963, pp. 215-217.

Kott, Jan. "*King Lear* and *Endgame*," *Shakespeare Our Contemporary*. London: Methuen, 1964.

Lebesque, Morvan. "Le Théâtre aux enfers: Artaud, Beckett et quelques autres," *Antonin Artaud et le théâtre de notre temps*. Paris: René Julliard, 1958, pp. 191-196.

LeSage, Laurent. "Samuel Beckett." *The French New Novel*. University Park: Pennsylvania State University Press, 1962, pp. 47-54. [About *Molloy* and *Malone Dies*.]

Levi, Albert W. *Literature, Philosophy and the Imagination*. Bloomington: Indiana University Press, 1963, p. 186.

Lewis, Allan. "The Theatre of the 'Absurd'—Beckett, Ionesco, Genêt." *The Contemporary Theatre*. New York: Crown, 1962, pp. 259-281.

Lumley, Frederick. "The Case Against Beckett." In *Trends in Twentieth Century Drama*. London: Rockliff, 1956, pp. 202-208.

MacNeice, Louis. *Varieties of Parable*. London: Cambridge University Press, 1965, pp. 119-129, 140-143.

Magill, Frank N., ed. *Cyclopedia of World Authors*. New York: Harper, 1958, pp. 84-86.

Mailer, Norman. "A Public Notice on *Waiting for Godot*." *Advertisements for Myself*. New York: G. P. Putnam's Sons, 1959, pp. 320-325. Reprinted in *Casebook on Waiting for Godot*, edited by Ruby Cohn. New York: Grove Press, 1967, pp. 69-74.

Mauriac, Claude. "Samuel Beckett." *The New Literature*. Translated by Samuel I. Stone. New York: Braziller, 1959, pp. 75-90.

Monnier, Adrienne. *Dernières gazettes et écrits divers*. Paris: Mercure de France, 1961.

Moore, Harry Thornton. "The Literature of the Absurd." *Twentieth Century French Literature Since World War II.* Carbondale: Southern Illinois University Press, 1966, pp. 147-176.

Mueller, William R. See Jacobsen, Josephine.

Nadeau, Maurice. "Samuel Beckett, l'humour et le néant." *La Littérature présente.* Paris: Corrêa, 1952, pp. 274-279.

Peyre, Henri. *The Contemporary French Novel.* New York: Oxford University Press, 1955, pp. 307-308.

Picon, Gaëton. *Panorama de la nouvelle littérature française.* Paris: Gallimard, 1960, pp. 157-159.

Poulet, Robert. "Samuel Becket [sic]." *La Lanterne magique.* Paris: Debresse, 1958, pp. 236-242.

Pritchett, V. S. "An Irish Oblomov." *The Living Novel and Later Appreciations.* New York: Random House, 1964, pp. 315-320.

Pronko, Leonard C. "Samuel Beckett." *Avant-Garde: The Experimental Theatre in France.* Berkeley: University of California Press, 1962, pp. 22-58.

————. "Theater and Anti-Theater." *Avant-Garde: The Experimental Theatre in France.* Berkeley: University of California Press, 1962, pp. 112-153.

Rexroth, Kenneth. "The Point Is Irrelevance." *On Contemporary Literature*, edited by Richard Kostelanetz. New York: Avon Books, 1964, pp. 244-248.

————. "Samuel Beckett and the Importance of Waiting."
Bird in the Bush. New York: New Directions, 1959,
pp. 75-85.

Robbe-Grillet, Alain. "Samuel Beckett, or Presence on the
Stage." *For a New Novel.* Translated by Richard Howard.
New York: Grove Press, 1966, pp. 111-125. Reprinted
in *Casebook on Waiting for Godot*, edited by Ruby Cohn.
New York: Grove Press, 1967, pp. 15-21.

Rousseaux, André. "L'Homme desintégré de Samuel Beckett."
Littérature du vingtième siècle. Paris: Albin Michel,
1955, pp. 105-113.

Rowe, Kenneth T. *A Theatre in Your Head.* New York:
Funk and Wagnalls, 1960, pp. 242-243.

Schramm, Ulf. *Fiktion und Reflexion: Uberlegungen zu Musil
und Beckett.* Frankfurt: Suhrkamp, 1967.

Scott, Nathan A., Jr. *Man in the Modern Theatre.* Richmond:
Knox, 1965, pp. 76-97.

Serreau, Genevieve. "Beckett's Clowns." *Histoire du Nouveau
Theatre.* Paris: Editions Gallimard, 1966. Reprinted
and translated from the French in *Casebook on Waiting
for Godot*, edited by Ruby Cohn. New York: Grove Press,
1967, pp. 171-175.

Shedd, Robert G. See Block, Haskell M.

Styan, J. L. *The Dark Comedy.* Cambridge: The University
Press, 1962, pp. 227-229.

Tallmer, Jerry. "Godot on Broadway" and "Godot: Still
Waiting." In *Village Voice Reader*, edited by Daniel Wolf

and Edwin Fancer. New York: Doubleday, 1962.
Reprinted by Grove Press, 1963, pp. 60-66.

Tynan, Kenneth. *"Fin de partie* and *Acte Sans paroles."*
Curtains. New York: Atheneum, 1961, pp. 401-403.

———. *"Krapp's Last Tape* and *Endgame." Curtains.*
New York: Atheneum, 1961, pp. 225-228.

———. *Tynan on Theatre.* New York: Atheneum, 1961,
pp. 36-38.

———. *"Waiting for Godot,* by Samuel Beckett at the Arts."
Curtains. New York: Atheneum, 1961, pp. 101-103.

———. *"Waiting for Godot,* by Samuel Beckett at the Golden."
Curtains. New York: Atheneum, 1961, p. 272.

Wellershoff, Dieter. *Der Gleichgültige: Versuche über
Hemingway, Camus, Benn, und Beckett.* Koln:
Kiepenheuer & Witsch, 1963.

Wellwarth, G. E. "The French-Speaking Drama: Samuel
Beckett." *The Theatre of Protest and Paradox.* New York:
New York University Press, 1964, pp. 37-51.

Whitehead, Frank. "Postscript: The Nineteen-Fifties." In A. S.
Collins, *English Literature of the Twentieth Century.*
London: University Tutorial Press, 1960, pp. 378-380.

Whittick, Arnold. *Symbols, Signs and Their Meaning.* London:
Leonard Hill, 1960, pp. 327-374.

Williams, Raymond. *Modern Tragedy.* London: Chatto
& Windus, 1966, pp. 153-155.

Wilson, Colin. *The Strength to Dream: Literature and the Imagination.* Boston: Houghton Mifflin Co., 1962, pp. 86-91.

Zeltner-Neukomm, Gerda. "Die lyrische Burleske." *Das Wagnis des französischen Gegenwartsromans—Die neue Welterfahrung in der Literatur.* Hamburg: Rowohlt, 1960, pp. 139-152.

D. Articles About Beckett

A., S. "Balzac a-t-il inspiré *En Attendant Godot?*" *Le Figaro Littéraire*, 17 September 1955, p. 12.

Abel, Lionel. "Joyce the Father, Beckett the Son." *New Leader*, 14 December 1959, pp. 26-27.

Abirached, Robert. "La Voix tragique de Samuel Beckett." *Etudes*, CCCXX (1964), 85-88.

Alpaugh, David J. "Negative Definition in Samuel Beckett's *Happy Days.*" *Twentieth Century Literature*, XI (1966), 202-210.

————. "The Symbolic Structure of Samuel Beckett's *All that Fall.*" *Modern Drama*, IX (1966), 324-332.

Alter, André. "*En attendant Godot* n'était pas une impasse— Beckett le prouve dans sa seconde pièce." *Le Figaro Littéraire*, 12 January 1957, pp. 1, 4.

Angus, William. "Modern Theatre Reflects the Times." *Queen's Quarterly*, LXX (Summer 1963), 255-263.

Ashmore, Jerome. "Philosophical Aspects of *Godot.*" *Symposium*, XVI (Winter 1962), 296-304.

28

Ashworth, Arthur. "New Theatre: Ionesco, Beckett, Pinter." *Southerly*, XXII (1962), 145-154.

Astre, Georges-Albert. "Notes." *Critique*, XIX (November 1963), 1020-1021.

Atkins, Anselm. "A Note on the Structure of Lucky's Speech." *Modern Drama*, IX (1966), 309.

Bachmann, Claus-Henning. "Die Hoffnung am Strick-Notizen zu Beckett und Béjart." *Antares*, VI (May 1958), 207-210.

Bajini, Sandro. "Beckett o l'emblema totale." *Il Verri*, III (April 1959), 70-88.

Ball, Patricia M. "Browning's Godot." *Victorian Poetry*, III (1965), 245-253.

Barbour, T. "Beckett and Ionesco." *Hudson Review*, XI (Summer 1958), 271-277.

Barjon, Louis. "Le Dieu de Beckett." *Études*, CCCXXII (January 1965), 650-662.

Barrett, William. "How I Understand Less and Less Every Year." *Columbia University Forum*, II (Winter 1959), 44-48.

―――. "The Works of Samuel Beckett Hold Clues for an Intriguing Riddle." *Saturday Review*, XL (8 June 1957), 15-16.

Barthes, Roland. "Le Théâtre français d'avant-garde." *Le Français dans le Monde*, no. 2 (June-July 1961), pp. 10-15.

Bataille, Georges. "Le Silence de Molloy." *Critique*, VII (15 May 1951), 387-396.

Beckett, Jeremy. "Compte rendu de *Waiting for Godot*." *Meanjin*, XV (Winter 1956), 216-218.

Benitez Claros, Rafael. "Teatro europeo del existencialismo al antiteatro." *Revisita de la Universidad de Madrid*, no. 34 (1960), pp. 235-254.

Bentley, Eric. "The Talent of Samuel Beckett." *New Republic*, CXXXIV (14 May 1956), 20-21. Reprinted in *Casebook on Waiting for Godot*, edited by Ruby Cohn. New York: Grove Press, 1967, pp. 59-66.

Berlin, Normand. "Beckett and Shakespeare." *French Review*, XL (1967), 647-651.

Bersani, Leo. "No Exit for Beckett." *Partisan Review*, XXXIII (1966), 261-267.

Bialos, Anne. "Samuel Beckett." *Studies in Literature* (Brooklyn College, New York), I (Spring 1961).

Bjurström, C. G. "Samuel Beckett." *Bonniers Litterära Magasin* (Sweden), XXIII (January 1954), 27-33.

Blanchot, Maurice. "Ou maintenant? Qui Maintenant?" *Nouvelle Revue Française*, II (October 1953), 676-686. Reprinted in *Le Livre à Venir*. Paris: Gallimard, 1959, pp. 256-264.

————. "A Rose Is a Rose...." *Nouvelle Revue française*, XI (July 1963), 86-93.

————. "Samuel Beckett." *Merkur*, no. 168 (February 1962), pp. 143-150.

————. "Where Now? Who Now?" *Evergreen Review*, II (Winter 1959), 222-229.

Blanzat, Jean. "Les Romans de Samuel Beckett." *Le Figaro Littéraire*, 13 May 1961, p. 2.

Blau, Herbert. " 'Meanwhile Follow the Bright Angels.' " *Tulane Drama Review*, V (September 1960), 89-101.

————. "The Popular, the Absurd and the *Entente Cordiale*." *Tulane Drama Review*, V (March 1961), 119-151.

Bollnow, Otto Friedrich. "Samuel Beckett." *Antares*, IV (March 1956), 31-36; IV (April 1956), 36-38; IV (June 1956), 42-43.

Bonczek, Jane C. "Being and Waiting: A Sign of our Times." *Lit*, no. 5 (1964), pp. 6-10.

Bonnefoi, Geneviève. "Textes pour rien?" *Les Lettres Nouvelles*, no. 36 (March 1956), 424-430.

Bowles, Patrick. "How Samuel Beckett Sees the Universe." *Listener*, LIX (19 June 1958), 1011-1012.

Bray, J. J. "The Hamm Funeral." *Meanjin*, XX (March 1962), 32-34.

Brée, Germaine. "Beckett's Abstractors of Quintessence." *French Review*, XXXVI (May 1963), 567-576.

————. "L'Etrange monde des 'grands articulés.' " *La Revue des lettres modernes*, no. 100 (1964), pp. 83-98.

Brick, Allan. "The Madman in His Cell: Joyce, Beckett, Nabokov and the Stereotypes." *Massachusetts Review*, I (October 1959), 40-55.

———. "A Note on Perception and Communication in Beckett's *Endgame.*" *Modern Drama*, IV (May 1961), 20-22.

Briggs, Ray. "Samuel Beckett's World in Waiting." *Saturday Review*, XL (8 June 1957), 14.

Brooke-Rose, Christine. "Samuel Beckett and the Anti-Novel." *London Magazine*, V (December 1958), 38-46.

Brooks, Curtis M. "The Mythic Pattern in *Waiting for Godot.*" *Modern Drama*, IX (1966), 292-299.

Brousse, Jacques. "Theater in Paris." *The European* (December 1953), pp. 39-43.

Brown, John Russell. "Mr. Beckett's Shakespeare." *Critical Quarterly*, V (Winter 1963), 310-326.

———. "Mr. Pinter's Shakespeare." *Critical Quarterly*, V (Autumn 1963), 251-265.

Brown, Robert McAfee. "The Theme of Waiting in Modern Literature." *Ramparts*, III (Summer 1964), 68-75.

Büchler, Franz. "Notizen zum Werk Samuel Becketts." *Die Neue Rundschau*, LXXV (1964), 482-487.

Burgess, Anthony. "Enduring Saturday." *Spectator*, CCXVI (29 April 1966), 532-533.

Butler, Harry L. "Balzac and Godeau, Beckett and Godot: A Curious Parallel." *Romance Notes*, III (Spring 1962), 13-17.

Butler, Michael. "Anatomy of Despair." *Encore*, VIII (May-June 1961), 17-24.

32

Cahiers de la Compagnie Madeleine Renaud—Jean-Louis Barrault, no. 44 (1963). (Special Beckett Issue).

Calendoli, Giovanni. "Il giuoco di Beckett al margine dell'ermetismo." La Fiera Letteraria, 21 September 1958, p. 1.

――――. "Personaggi atomizzati nel teatro di Beckett." La Fiera Letteraria, 1 October 1961, p. 1.

Cambon, Glauco. "Immediacies and Distances." Poetry, xcv (March 1960), 379-381.

Cami, Ben. "Lawrence Durrell: Een Paar Nota's." De Vlaamse Gids, xlii (October 1958), 635-637.

Case, Sue-Ellen. "Image and Godot." In Casebook on Waiting for Godot, edited by Ruby Cohn. New York: Grove Press, 1967. pp. 155-159.

Cavanagh, Maura. "Waiting for God. Parody." Audience, v (Summer 1958), 94-114.

Chadwick, C. "Waiting for Godot: A Logical Approach." Symposium, xiv (Winter 1960), 252-257.

Chambers, Ross. "Beckett's Brinkmanship." Journal of the Australasian Universities Language and Literature Association, no. 19 (1963), pp. 57-75.

――――. "Samuel Beckett and the Padded Cell." Meanjin, xxi (1962), 451-462.

――――. "Samuel Beckett, homme des situations limités." Cahiers de la Compagnie Madeleine Renaud— Jean-Louis Barrault, no. 44 (1963), pp. 37-62.

————. "Vers une interprétation de *Fin de partie*." *Studi Francesi*, XI (1967), 90-96.

Champigny, R. "Les aventures de la première personne." *La Revue des lettres modernes*, no. 100 (1964), pp. 117-130.

————. "Interpretation d'*En attendant Godot*." *PMLA*, LXXV (June 1960), 329-331.

Chapsal, Madeleine. "Un célèbre inconnu." *L'Express*, 8 February 1957, pp. 26-27.

————. "Le jeune roman." *L'Express*, 12 January 1961, p. 31.

Chase, N. C. "Images of Man: *Le Malentendu* and *En attendant Godot*." *Wisconsin Studies in Contemporary Literature*, VII (1966), 295-302.

Chaucer, Daniel. "*Waiting for Godot*." *Shenandoah* (Spring 1955), 80-82.

Chiaromonte, Nicola. "Beckett e la fine del mondo." *Il Mondo*, X (16 September 1958), 14.

Christie, Erling. "Det absurde drama. Tanker omkring Samuel Beckett's *Waiting for Godot*." *Samtiden*, LXVI (1957), 578-584.

Cimatti, Pietro. "Beckett uomo zero." *La Fiera Letteraria*, 12 January 1958, p. 2.

————. "L'Ironia di Becckett." *La Fiera Letteraria*, 6 March 1960, pp. 1-2.

Clements, J. "Samuel Beckett's Bilingualism: A Comparative Study of *En attendant Godot* and *Waiting for Godot*." Master's thesis, University of Indiana, 1961.

Closs, August. "Formprobleme und Möglichkeiter zur Gestaltung der Tragödie in der Gegenwart." *Stil-und-Formprobleme*, [v] (1960), 483-491.

Clurman, Harold. "Theater." *Nation*, CLXXXII (5 May 1956), 387-390.

Cmarada, Geraldine. "*Malone Dies*: A Round on Consciousness." *Symposium*, XIV (Fall 1960), 199-212.

Codignola, Luciano. "Il Grigio di Beckett." *Il Mondo*, XIII (13 June 1961), 14.

————. "Il teatro della guerra fredda—3. Samuel Beckett." *Tempo Presente*, II (January 1957), 53-56.

Coe, Richard N. "Le Dieu de Samuel Beckett." *Cahiers de la Compagnie Madeleine Renaud—Jean-Louis Barrault*, no. 44 (1963), pp. 6-36.

————. "God and Samuel Beckett." *Meanjin*, XXIV (1965), 66-85.

Coffey, Brian. "Memory's Murphy Maker: Some Notes on Samuel Beckett." *Threshold*, no. 17, n.d., pp. 28-36.

Cohen, Robert S. "Parallels and the Possibility of Influence Between Simone Weil's *Waiting for God* and Samuel Beckett's *Waiting for Godot.*" *Modern Drama*, VI (February 1964), 425-436.

Cohn, Ruby. "The Absurdly Absurd: Avatars of Godot." *Comparative Literature Studies*, II (1965), 233-240.

————. "Acting for Beckett." *Modern Drama*, IX (1966), 237.

———. "The Beginnings of *Endgame.*" *Modern Drama*, IX (1966), 319-323.

———. "Comedy of Samuel Beckett: Something Old, Something New. . . ." *Yale French Studies*, no. 23 (1959), pp. 11-17.

———. "*Comment c'est*: *De quoi rive.*" *French Review*, XXV (1962), 563-569.

———. "Joyce and Beckett, Irish Cosmopolitans." *Proceedings of the Fourth Congress of the International Comparative Literature Association*, edited by François Jost. Vol. I. The Hague: Mouton, 1966, 109-113.

———. "Note on Beckett, Dante, and Geulincx." *Comparative Literature*, XII (Winter 1960), 93-94.

———. "Philosophical Fragments in the Works of Samuel Beckett." *Criticism*, VI (1964), 33-43.

———. "Play and Player in the Plays of Samuel Beckett." *Yale French Studies*, no. 29 (1962), pp. 43-48.

———. "The Plays of Yeats through Beckett-Coloured Glasses." *Threshold*, no. 19 (Autumn 1965), pp. 41-47.

———. "Preliminary Observations." *Perspective*, XI (Autumn 1959), 119-131.

———. "Samuel Beckett, Self-Translator." *PMLA*, LXXVI (December 1961), 613-621.

———. "Samuel Beckett: The Comic Gamut." *Dissertation Abstracts*, XXI (1961), 2711-2712.

————. "Still Novel." *Yale French Studies*, no. 24 (1959), pp. 48-53.

————. "Tempest in an Endgame." *Symposium*, XIX (Winter 1965), 328-334.

————. " 'Theatrum Mundi' and Contemporary Theatre." *Comparative Drama*, I (Spring 1967), 28-35.

————. "Waiting Is All," *Modern Drama*, III (September 1960), 162-167.

————. "*Watt* in the Light of *The Castle*." *Comparative Literature*, XIII (Spring 1961), 154-166.

Cole, Connelly. "A Note on *Waiting for Godot*." *Icarus* (January 1957), pp. 25-27.

Cooney, Séamus. "Beckett's *Murphy*." *Explicator*, XXV (1966), Item 3.

Corrigan, Robert W. "The Theatre in Search of a Fix." *Tulane Drama Review*, V (June 1961), 21-35.

Craig, H.A.L. "Poetry in the Theatre." *New Statesman and Nation*, 12 November 1960, pp. 734-736.

Cunrad, Nancy. "The Hours Press." *Book Collector*, XIII (Winter 1964), 488-496.

Curtis, Anthony. "Mood of the Month—IV." *London Magazine*, V (May 1958), 60-65.

Curtis, Jean-Louis. "La voix qui babille dans le désert." *Cahiers des saisons*, no. 36 (Winter 1964), pp. 105-106.

Damiens, Claude. "Regards sur le 'theatre nouveau': Beckett, Ionesco, Genêt, Duras, Adamov." *Paris-Théâtre*, no. 173 (1961), pp. 12-13.

D'Aubarède, Gabriel. "Waiting for Beckett." *Trace*, no. 42 (Summer 1961), pp. 156-158.

Davenport, Guy. "Beckett and Kenner, Tandem." *National Review*, XII (8 May 1962), 330-332.

Davie, Donald. "Kinds of Comedy." *Spectrum*, II (Winter 1958), 25-31.

Davin, Dan. "Mr. Beckett's Everymen." *Irish Writing*, no. 34 (Spring 1956), pp. 36-39.

Deming, Barbara. "John Osborne's War Against the Philistines." *Hudson Review*, XI (Autumn 1958), 411-419.

Dennis, Nigel. "No View from the Toolshed." *Encounter*, XX (January 1963), 37-39.

De Stefano, Sister Mary Venise. "Man's Search for Meaning in Modern French Drama." *Renascence* (Winter 1964), pp. 81-91.

Devlin, Denis. "Samuel Beckett." *Transition*, no. 27 (April-May 1938), pp. 289-294.

Dobrée, Bonamy. "The London Theater, 1957: The Melting Pot." *Sewanee Review*, LXVI (Winter 1958), 146-160. [About *Fin de Partie*.]

Dort, Bernard. "*En attendant Godot*, pièce de Samuel Beckett." *Les Temps modernes*, VIII (May 1953), 1842-1845.

———. "Sur une avant-garde: Adamov et quelques autres." *Théâtre d'Aujourd'hui*, no. 3 (September-October 1957), pp. 13-16.

Dreyfus, Dina. "Vraies et fausses énigmes." *Mercure de France*, CCCXXXI (October 1957), 268-285.

Driver, Tom F. "Beckett by the Madeleine." *Columbia University Forum*, IV (Summer 1961), 21-25.

Dubois, Jacques. "Beckett and Ionesco: The Tragic Awareness of Pascal and the Ironic Awareness of Flaubert." *Modern Drama*, IX (1966), 283-291.

Duckworth, Colin. "The Making of *Godot*." *Theatre Research*, VII (1966), 123-145. Reprinted in *Casebook on Waiting for Godot*, edited by Ruby Cohn. New York: Grove Press, 1967, pp. 89-100.

Dukore, Bernard F. "Beckett's Play, *Play*." *Educational Theatre Journal*, XVII (1965), 19-23.

———. "Controversy: A Non-Interpretation of *Godot*." *Drama Survey*, III (1963), 117-119.

———. "Gogo, Didi, and the Absent Godot." *Drama Survey*, I (1962), 301-307.

Dumur, Guy. "Les Métamorphoses du théâtre d'avant-garde (à propos de cinq reprises récentes)." *Théâtre Populaire*, no. 42 (2ᵉ trim., 1961), pp. 100-106.

Easthope, A. "Hamm, Clov, and Dramatic Method in *Endgame*." *Modern Drama*, X (February 1968), 424-433.

Eastman, Richard M. "The Open Parable: Demonstration and Definition." *College English*, XXII (October 1960), 15-18.

——. "Samuel Beckett and *Happy Days.*" *Modern Drama*, VI (February 1964), 417-424.

——. "The Strategy of Samuel Beckett's *Endgame.*" *Modern Drama*, II (May 1959), 36-44.

Edström, Mauritz. "Ansiket pa väggen." *Ord och Bild*, LXXV (1966), 19-24.

Ellman, Richard M. "Beckett's Testament." *Commonweal*, LXXX (26 June 1964), 416-418.

Erickson, John D. "Objects and Systems in the Novels of Samuel Beckett." *L'Esprit Créateur*, VII (1967), 113-122.

Esslin, Martin. "The Absurdity of the Absurd." *Kenyon Review*, XXII (Fall 1960), 670-673.

——. "Godot and his Children: The Theatre of Samuel Beckett and Harold Pinter." *Experimental Drama*, XIV (1964), 128-146.

——. "The Theatre of the Absurd." *Tulane Drama Review*, IV (May 1960), 3-15.

Fabre, Pierre. "Beckett et Borgès—Le Prix international des Éditeurs revient à des auteurs difficiles." *Carrefour*, no. 870 (17 May 1961), p. 25.

Fanizza, Franco. "La parola e il silenzio ne '*L'innommable*' di Samuel Beckett." *Aut Aut*, no. 60 (November 1960), pp. 380-391.

Fasano, Giancarlo. "Samuel Beckett." *Belfagor*, XVIII (1962), 433-457.

Federman, Raymond. "Beckett and the Fiction of Mud." *On Contemporary Literature.* New York: Avon, 1964, pp. 255-261.

—————. "Beckett's Belacqua and the Inferno of Society." *Arizona Quarterly*, XX (Autumn 1964), 231-241.

—————. "Le bonheur chez Samuel Beckett." *Esprit*, CCCLXII (1967), 90-96.

—————. " 'How It Is' with Beckett's Fiction." *French Review*, XXXVIII (1965), 459-468.

—————. "Samuel Beckett ou le bonheur en enfer." *Symposium*, XXI (Spring 1967), 14-21.

—————. "Samuel Beckett's Early Novels: From Social Reality to Fictional Absurdity." *Dissertation Abstracts*, XXIV (1963), 2030.

Fitch, Brian T. "Narrateur et narration dans la trilogie romanesque de Samuel Beckett: *Molloy, Malone Meurt, L'Innommable.*" *Bulletin des Jeunes Romanistes*, no. 3 (May 1961), pp. 13-20.

Fletcher, D. "Molloy for Prime Minister." *Left Wing* (November 1962), pp. 22-24.

Fletcher, John. "Action and Play in Beckett's Theatre." *Modern Drama*, IX (1966), 242-250.

—————. "Beckett and Balzac Revisited." *French Review* (October 1963), pp. 78-80.

———. "Beckett and the Fictional Tradition." *Caliban*, N.S., I (1965), 147-158.

———. "Beckett et Proust." *Caliban*, N.S., I (1964), 89-100.

———. "Beckett's Debt to Dante." *Nottingham French Studies*, IV (1965), 41-52.

———. "Beckett's Verse: Influences and Parallels." *French Review*, XXXVII (1964), 320-331.

———. "Roger Blin at Work." *Modern Drama*, VIII (1966), 403-408. Reprinted in *Casebook on Waiting for Godot*, edited by Ruby Cohn. New York: Grove Press, 1967, pp. 21-26.

———. "Samuel Beckett and the Philosophers." *Comparative Literature*, XVII (1965), 42-56.

———. "Samuel Beckett as Critic." *Listener*, LXXIV (November 1965), 862-863.

———. "Samuel Beckett et Jonathan Swift: Vers une étude comparée." *Littératures X* (Toulouse), XI (1962), i, 81-117.

———. "Samuel Beckett; or, the Morbid Dread of Sphinxes." *New Durham* (June 1965), pp. 5-9.

Flood, Ethelbert. "A Reading of Beckett's *Godot*." *Culture*, XII (1961), 357-362.

Fournier, Edith. "Pour que la boue me soit contée. . . ." *Critique*, no. 168 (May 1961), pp. 412-418.

42

Fowlie, Wallace. "New French Theatre: Artaud, Beckett, Genêt, Ionesco." *Sewanee Review*, LXVII (Fall 1959), 648-651.

Francis, Richard Lee. "Beckett's Metaphysical Tragicomedy." *Modern Drama*, VIII (1965), 259-267.

Frank, Nino. "Scherzi di Becket [sic]." *Il Mondo*, VII (4 October 1955), 10.

French, Judith Ann. "The Destruction of Action." *Kerygma*, III (Spring 1963), 9-12.

Friedman, Melvin J. "Achievement of Samuel Beckett." *Books Abroad*, XXXIII (Summer 1959), 278-281.

————. "Beckett Criticism: Its Early Prime." *Symposium*, XXI (Spring 1967), 82-89.

————. "The Creative Writer as Polyglot: Valéry, Larbaud, and Samuel Beckett." *Wisconsin Academy of Sciences, Arts, and Letters*, XLIX (1960), 229-236.

————. "Critic!" *Modern Drama*, IX (1966), 300-308.

————. "Molloy's 'Sacred' Stones." *Romance Notes*, IX (1967), 8-11.

————. "A Note on Leibniz and Samuel Beckett." *Romance Notes*, IV (Spring 1963), 93-96.

————. "Novels of Samuel Beckett: An Amalgam of Joyce and Proust." *Comparative Literature*, XII (Winter 1960), 47-58.

————. "Préface." *La Revue des lettres modernes*, no. 100 (1964), pp. 10-21.

————. "Les Romans de Samuel Beckett et la tradition du grotesque." *La Revue des lettres modernes*, no. 100 (1964), pp. 31-50.

————. "Samuel Beckett and the 'nouveau roman.'" *Wisconsin Studies in Contemporary Literature*, I (Spring-Summer 1960), 22-36.

Frisch, Jack E. "*Endgame*: A Play as Poem." *Drama Survey*, III (Fall 1963), 257-263.

————. "Ironic Theatre: Techniques of Irony in the Plays of Samuel Beckett, Eugène Ionesco, Harold Pinter, and Jean Gênet." *Dissertation Abstracts*, XXV (1965), 6114-6115.

Frye, Northrup. "The Nightmare Life in Death." *Hudson Review*, XIII (Autumn 1960), 442-449.

Furbank, P. N. "Beckett's Purgatory." *Encounter*, XXII (1964), 69-72.

Gassner, John. "Broadway in Review." *Educational Theatre Journal*, X (May 1958), 122-131.

Gattnig, C. J., Jr. "Pirandello, Umorismo, and Beckett." *Dissertation Abstracts*, XXVIII (1968), 3807-A.

Geerts, Leo. "Samuel Beckett vertaald: De dramatiek van de herinnering." *Dietsche Warande en Belfort*, CXII (1967), 533-538.

Gênet, Jean. "Letter from Paris." *New Yorker*, XXXVII (4 March 1961), 95-100.

Gerard, Martin. "Molloy Becomes Unnamable." *X, A Quarterly Review*, I (October 1960), 314-319.

Glicksberg, Charles I. "Forms of Madness in Literature." *Arizona Quarterly*, XVII (Spring 1961), 42-53.

―――. "The Lost Self in Modern Literature." *Personalist*, XLIII (August 1962), 527-538.

―――. "Samuel Beckett's World of Fiction." *Arizona Quarterly*, XVIII (Spring 1962), 32-47.

Gold, Herbert. "Beckett: Style and Desire." *Nation*, 10 November 1956, pp. 397-399.

Goldberg, Gerald Jay. "The Search for the Artist in Some Recent British Fiction." *South Atlantic Quarterly* (Summer 1963), pp. 387-401.

Gordon, L. G. "Dialectic of the Beast and Monk: The Dramatic Rhetoric of Samuel Beckett." *Dissertation Abstracts*, XXVIII (1967), 1077-A.

Gorelick, Mordecai. "An Epic Theatre Catechism." *Tulane Drama Review*, IV (September 1959), 90-95.

Gouhier, Henri. "Le théâtre a horreur du vide." *La Table Ronde*, no. 182 (March 1963), pp. 120-124.

Gray, Ronald. "*Waiting for Godot*: A Christian Interpretation." *Listener*, LVII (24 January 1957), 160-161.

Greenberg, Alvin. "The Death of the Psyche: A Way to the Self in the Contemporary Novel." *Criticism*, VIII (1966), 1-18.

Gregory, Horace. "Beckett's Dying Gladiators." *Commonweal*, LXV (29 October 1956), 325-328.

————. "Prose and Poetry of Samuel Beckett." *Commonweal*, LXXI (30 October 1959), 162-163.

Grenier, Jean. "*En attendant Godot.*" *Le disque vert*, I (July-August 1953), 81-86.

Gresset, Michel. "Création et cruauté chez Beckett." *Tel Quel*, no. 15 (1963), pp. 58-65.

————. "Le 'parce que' chez Faulkner et le 'donc' chez Beckett." *Les Lettres nouvelles*, IX (November 1961), 124-138.

Grillandi, Massimo. "Samuel Beckett." *L'Italia che Scrive*, XLIV (July-August 1961), 147-148.

Grillo, Guiseppe. "Samuel Beckett fra anti-teatro e anti-romanzo." *Idea*, XVI (1960), 698-700.

Gross, John. "Amazing Reductions." *Encounter*, XXIII (September 1964), 51-52.

Guicharnaud, Jacques. "The 'R' Effect." *L'Esprit créateur*, II (Winter 1962), 159-165.

Hafley, James. "The Human Image in Contemporary Art." *Kerygma*, III (Spring 1963), 25-34.

Hainsworth, J. D. "Shakespeare, Son of Beckett." *Modern Language Quarterly*, XXV (1964), 346-355.

Halldén, Ruth; Ingemar Hedenius; and Sandro Key-Åberg. "Ettsamtal om Samuel Beckett." *Ord och Bild*, LXXII (1963), 93-104.

Hambro, Carl. "Samuel Becketts 'romantrilogi.'" *Vinduet*, XVIII (1964), 9-14.

Hamilton, Carol. "Portrait in Old Age: The Image of Man in Beckett's Trilogy." *Western Humanities Review*, XVI (Spring 1962), 157-165.

Hamilton, Kenneth. "Boon or Thorn? Joyce Cary and Samuel Beckett on Human Life." *Dalhousie Review*, XXXVIII (Winter 1959), 433-442.

————. "Negative Salvation in Samuel Beckett." *Queen's Quarterly*, LXIX (Spring 1962), 102-111.

Hampton, Charles Christy. "The Human Situation in the Plays of Samuel Beckett: A Study in Stratagems of Inaction." *Dissertation Abstracts*, XXVII (1966), 206A.

Hansen-Löve, Friedrich. "Samuel Beckett oder die Einübung ins Nichts." *Hochland*, L (October 1957), 36-46.

Hartley, Anthony. "Samuel Beckett." *Spectator*, CXCI (23 October 1953), 458-459.

Harvey, Lawrence E. "Art and the Existential in *En attendant Godot*." *PMLA*, LXXV (March 1960), 137-146. Reprinted in *Casebook on Waiting for Godot*, edited by Ruby Cohn. New York: Grove Press, 1967, pp. 144-154.

————. "Samuel Beckett: initiation du poète." *La Revue des lettres modernes*, no. 100 (1964), pp. 153-168.

————. "Samuel Beckett on Life, Art, and Criticism." *Modern Language Notes*, LXXX (1965), 545-562.

Hassan, Ihab. "The Literature of Silence: From Henry Miller to Beckett and Burroughs." *Encounter*, XXVIII (January 1967), 74-82.

Hatch, Robert. "Laughter at Your Own Risk." *Horizon*, III (September 1960), 112-116.

Hayman, David. Introduction to an Extract from *The Unnamable*, *Texas Quarterly*, I (Spring 1958), 127-128.

————. "Molloy à la recherche de l'absurde." *La Revue des lettres modernes*, no. 100 (1964), pp. 131-151.

Hedenius, Ingemar. See Halldén, Ruth.

Hesla, David H. "The Shape of Chaos: A Reading of Beckett's *Watt*." *Critique*, VI (Spring 1963), 85-105.

————. "The Shape of Chaos: An Interpretation of the Art of Samuel Beckett." Ph.D. dissertation, University of Chicago, 1964.

Hesse, Eva. "Die Welt des Samuel Beckett." *Akzente*, VIII (1961), 244-266.

Hewes, Henry. "Mankind in the Merdecluse." *Saturday Review*, 5 May 1956. Reprinted in *Casebook on Waiting for Godot*, edited by Ruby Cohn. New York: Grove Press, 1967, pp. 67-69.

Hicks, Granville. "Beckett's World." *Saturday Review* (4 October 1958), p. 14.

Hobson, Harold. "Samuel Beckett, Dramatist of the Year." *International Theatre Annual No. I*. New York: Citadel Press, 1956, pp. 153-155.

Hoefer, Jacqueline. "*Watt*." *Perspective*, XI (Autumn 1959), 166-182.

Hoffman, Frederick J. "L'Insaisissable moi: Les 'M' de Samuel Beckett." *La Revue des lettres modernes*, no. 100 (1964), pp. 23-53.

Hofstadter, Albert. "The Tragicomic: Concern in Depth." *Journal of Aesthetics and Art Criticism*, XXIV (Winter 1965), 295-302.

Hooker, Ward. "Irony and Absurdity in the Avant-Garde Theatre." *Kenyon Review*, XXII (Summer 1960), 436-454.

Hubert, Renée Riese. "Beckett's *Play* Between Poetry and Performance." *Modern Drama*, IX (1966), 339-346.

————. "The Couple and the Performance in Samuel Beckett's Plays." *L'Esprit Créateur*, II (Winter 1962), 175-180.

Hughes, Catherine. "Beckett and the Game of Life." *Catholic World*, CXCV (June 1962), 163-168.

————. "Beckett's World: Wherein God Is Continually Silent." *Critic*, XX (April-May 1962), 40-42.

Hughes, D. A. "The Work of Samuel Beckett." *Humanist*, LXXXII (September 1967), 271-275.

Hughes, Daniel J. "Reality and the Hero." *Modern Fiction Studies*, VI (Winter 1960-1961), 345-364.

Iser, Wolfgang. "Samuel Beckett's Dramatic Language." *Modern Drama*, IX (1966), 251-259.

————. "Samuel Becketts dramatische Sprache." *Germanisch-romanisch Monatsschrift*, XLII (1961), 451-467.

Jacobsen, Josephine, and William R. Mueller. "Beckett as Poet." *Prairie Schooner*, xxxvii (1963), 196-216.

Janvier, Ludovic. "Réduire à la parole." *Cahiers de la Compagnie Madeleine Renaud—Jean-Louis Barrault*, lIII (1966), 42-48.

Jessup, Bertram. "About Beckett, Godot and Others." *Northwest Review*, i (Spring 1956), 23-28.

Johnston, Denis. "Waiting with Beckett." *Irish Writing*, no. 34 (Spring 1956), pp. 23-28.

Josbin, Raoul. "Chronique du théâtre." *Etudes*, no. 150 (July-August 1953), pp. 77-83.

Kaiser, Joachim. "Am Rande dessen, was sagbar is Zum 60, Geburtstag des Dichters Samuel Beckett." *Universitas*, xxi (1966), 605-610.

Kaiser, Rudolf. "Vier Sonette." *Neueren Sprachen*, no. 6 (June 1963), pp. 252-262.

Karl, Frederick. "Waiting for Beckett: Quest and Re-Quest." *Sewanee Review*, lxix (Fall 1961), 661-676.

Kenner, Hugh. "The Absurdity of Fiction." *Griffin* (November 1959), pp. 13-16.

———. "Art in a Closed Field." *Virginia Quarterly Review*, xxxviii (1962), 597-613.

———. "The Beckett Landscape." *Spectrum*, ii (Winter 1958), 8-24.

———. "The Cartesian Centaur." *Perspective*, xi (Autumn 1959), 132-141.

————. "Samuel Beckett vs. Fiction." *National Review*, VI (11 October 1958), 248-249.

————. "Voices in the Night." *Spectrum*, V (Spring 1961), 3-20.

————. "Samuel Beckett: The Rational Domain." *Forum*, III (Summer 1960), 39-47.

Kermode, Frank. "Beckett, Snow, and Pure Poverty." *Encounter*, XV (July 1960), 73-77.

————. "The New Apocalyptists." *Partisan Review*, XXXIII (1966), 339-361.

Kern, Edith. "Beckett and the Spirit of the Commedia dell'Arte." *Modern Drama*, IX (1966), 260-267.

————. "Beckett's Knight of Infinite Resignation." *Yale French Studies*, no. 29 (1962), pp. 49-56.

————. "Concretization of Metaphor in the Commedia dell'Arte and the Modern Theatre." In *Proceedings of the Fourth Congress of the International Comparative Literature Association*, edited by François Jost. Den Haag: Mouton, 1966, pp. 1232-1242.

————. "Drama Stripped for Inaction: Beckett's *Godot*." *Yale French Studies*, no. 14 (1954-1955), pp. 41-47.

————. "Moran-Molloy: The Hero as Author." *Perspective*, XI (Autumn 1959), 183-193.

————. "Samuel Beckett—Dionysian Poet." *Descant*, III (Winter 1959), 33-36.

————. "Samuel Beckett et les poches de Gulliver." *La Revue des lettres modernes*, no. 100 (1964), pp. 69-82.

Kesting, Marianne. "Das Romanwerk Samuel Becketts." *Neue deutsche Hefte*, Heft 86 (1962), pp. 97-109.

Key-Åberg, Sandro. See Halldén, Ruth.

————. "Om absurdismen." *Ord och Bild*, LXXI (1962), 119-126.

Klawitterm, Robert Louis. "Being and Time in Samuel Beckett's Novels." *Dissertation Abstracts*, XXVI (1966), 7320.

Knight, G. Wilson. "The Kitchen Sink: On Recent Developments in Drama." *Encounter*, XXI (December 1963), 48-54.

Kolve, V. A. "Religious Language in *Waiting for Godot*." *The Centennial Review*, XI (1967), 102-127.

Kott, Jan. "*King Lear* or *Endgame*." *Evergreen Review*, no. 33 (August-September 1964), pp. 53-65.

————. "A Note on Beckett's Realism." *Tulane Drama Review*, X (1966), 156-159.

————. "*Le roi Lear*, autrement dit *Fin de partie*." *Temps modernes*, no. 194 (1962), pp. 48-77.

Krämer-Badoni, Rudolf. "Die Annihilierung des Nihilismus, ein Versuch über Samuel Beckett." *Forum* (Vienna), VIII (April 1961), 148-152.

Lamont, Rosette. "Death and Tragi-comedy: Three Plays of the New Theatre." *Massachusetts Review*, VI (1965), 381-402.

————. "La Farce métaphysique de Samuel Beckett." *La Revue des lettres modernes*, no. 100 (1964), pp. 99-116.

————. The Metaphysical Farce: Beckett and Ionesco." *French Review*, XXXII (1959), 319-328.

Lancelotti, Mario A. "Observaciones sobre *Molloy*." *Sur* (Argentina), no. 273 (November-December 1961), pp. 50-52.

Lappalainen, Armas. "Under Becketts presenning." *Ord och Bild*, LXXI (1962), 439-442.

Lee, Warren. "The Bitter Pill of Samuel Beckett." *Chicago Review*, X (Winter 1957), 77-87.

Leech, Clifford. "When Writing Becomes Absurd." *Colorado Quarterly*, XII (Summer 1964), 6-24.

Lees, F.N. "Samuel Beckett." *Membership and Proceedings, Manchester Literary and Philosophical Society*, CIV (1961-62), iv. [19 pp. off-print.]

LeHardouin, Maria. "L'Anti-héros, ou 'Richard n'aime plus Richard.'" *Synthèses*, no. 139 (December 1957), pp. 398-405.

Lemarchand, Jacques. "*Fin de parti* de Samuel Beckett, au Studio des Champs-Elysées." *Le Figaro Littéraire*, 11 May 1957, p. 14.

Lennon, Peter. "Beckett on Buster." *Manchester Guardian*, 19 February 1966, p. 6.

Leroux, Normand. "Pour Samuel Beckett." *Études Françaises*, III (1967), 240-243.

Leventhal, A.J. "The Beckett Hero." *Critique*, VII (1965), 18-35.

————. "Close of *Play*." *Dublin Magazine*, XXXII (April-June 1957), 18-22.

————. "Le Heros de Beckett." *Les Lettres Nouvelles*, (June 1964), pp. 305-312.

————. "Mr. Beckett's *En attendant Godot*." *Dublin Magazine*, (April-June 1954), pp. 11-16.

————. "Reflections on Samuel Beckett's New Work for the French Theatre." *Dublin Magazine*, XXXII (April-June 1957), 18-22.

————. "Samuel Beckett, Poet and Pessimist." *Listener*, LVII (9 May 1957), 746-747.

Levy, Alan. "The Long Wait for Godot." *Theatre Arts*, XL (August 1956), 33-35, 96. Reprinted in *Casebook on Waiting for Godot*, edited by Ruby Cohn. New York: Grove Press, 1967, pp. 74-78.

Lewis, Allan. "The Fun and Games of Edward Albee." *Educational Theatre Journal*, XVI (March 1964), 29-39.

Lodge, David. "Some Ping Understood." *Encounter*, XXX (February 1968), 85-89.

Loy, J. Robert. " 'Things' in Recent French Literature." *PMLA*, LXXI (1956), 27-41.

Ludvigsen, C. "Samuel Beckett." *Vindrosen*, VI (1959), 437-444.

Lyons, Charles R. "Beckett's *Endgame*: An Anti-Myth of Creation." *Modern Drama*, vii (September 1964), 204-209.

McCoy, Charles S. "*Waiting for Godot*: A Biblical Appraisal." *Religion in Life*, xxviii (Fall 1959), 595-603.

————. "*Waiting for Godot*: A Biblical Approach." *Florida Review*, no. 2 (Spring 1958), pp. 63-72.

Macksey, Richard. "The Artist in the Labyrinth: Design or Dasein." *Modern Language Notes*, lxxvii (May 1962), 239-256.

Mackworth, Cecily. "French Writing Today—Les Coupables." *Twentieth Century*, clxi (May 1957), 459-468.

Magnan, Jean-Marie. "Jalons i. Samuel Beckett ou les chaînes et relais du néant. ii. Alain Robbe-Grillet ou le labyrinthe du voyeur." *Cahiers du Sud*, l (1963), 73-80.

Magny, Olivier de. "Panorama d'une nouvelle littérature romanesque." *Esprit*, nos. 7-8 (July-August 1958), pp. 3-18.

————. "Samuel Beckett et la farce métaphysique." *Cahiers de la Compagnie Madeleine Renaud—Jean-Louis Barrault*, no. 44 (1963), pp. 67-72.

————. "Samuel Beckett ou Job abandonée." *Paru* (Monte Carlo), no. 97 (August 1956), pp. 92-99.

Maierhöfer, Fränzi. "Becketts forcierte Negation." *Stimmen der Zeit*, clxxx (1967), 105-119.

Mannes, Marya. "A Seat in the Stalls." *Reporter*, XIII (20 October 1955), 43.

Marcel, Gabriel. "Atomisation du théâtre." *Les Nouvelles Littéraires*, no. 1555 (20 June 1957), p. 10.

Marinello, Leone J. "Samuel Beckett's *Waiting for Godot*." *Drama Critique*, VI (Spring 1963), 75-81.

Markus, Thomas B. "Bernard Dukore and *Waiting for Godot*." *Drama Survey*, II (1963), 360-363.

Marmori, Giancarlo. "Il fango di Beckett." *Il Mondo*, XIII (March 1961), 15.

Marowitz, Charles. "A View from the Gods." *Encore*, X (January-February 1963), 6-7.

Marrissel, André. "L'Univers de Samuel Beckett: Un noeud de complexes." *Esprit*, XXXI (September 1963), 240-255.

Maulnier, Thierry. "De Beckett à Bernanos." *La Revue de Paris*, LXIV (June 1957), 139-142.

Mayoux, Jean-Jacques. "Beckett and Expressionism." *Modern Drama*, IX (1966), 238-241.

―――. "Beckett et l'humour." *Cahiers de la Compagnie Madeleine Renaud—Jean-Louis Barrault*, LIII (1967), 33-41.

―――. "Samuel Beckett et l'univers parodique." *Les Lettres Nouvelles*, no. 6 (August 1960), 271-291.

―――. "Le Théâtre de Samuel Beckett." *Etudes anglaises*, X (October-December 1957), 350-366.

56

————. "The Theatre of Samuel Beckett." *Perspective*, XI (Autumn 1959), 142-155.

Mercier, Vivian. "Arrival of the Anti-Novel." *Commonweal*, LXX (1960), 149-151.

————. "Beckett and the Search for Self." *New Republic*, CXXXIII (September 1955), 20-21.

————. "How to Read *Endgame*." *Griffin* (June 1959), pp. 10-14.

————. "The Mathematical Limit." *Nation*, CLXXXVIII (14 February 1959), 144-145.

————. "A Pyrrhonian Eclogue." *The Hudson Review*, VII (Winter 1955), 620-624.

————. "Samuel Beckett and the Sheela-na-gig." *Kenyon Review*, XXIII (Spring 1961), 299-325.

————. "Savage Humor." *Commonweal*, LXVI (17 May 1957), 188-190.

Metman, Eva. "Reflections on Samuel Beckett's Plays." *Journal of Analytical Psychology*, V (January 1960), 41-63.

Metz, Mary S. "Existentialism and Inauthenticity in the Theatre of Beckett, Ionesco, and Genêt." *Dissertation Abstracts*, XXVII (1966), 1377A-1378A.

Micha, René. "Une Nouvelle littérature allégorique." *Nouvelle Revue française*, III (April 1954), 696-706.

Middleton, Christopher. "Randnotizen zu den Romanen von Samuel Beckett." *Akzente*, IV (October 1957), 407-412.

Mihályi, Gábor. "Beckett's *Godot* and the Myth of Alienation." *Modern Drama*, IX (1966), 277-282.

Miller, J. Hillis. "The Anonymous Walkers." *Nation*, CXC (23 April 1960), 351-354.

Miller, Karl. "Beckett's Voices." *Encounter*, XIII (September 1959), 59-61.

Mintz, Samuel I. "Beckett's *Murphy*: A 'Cartesian' Novel." *Perspective*, XI (Autumn 1959), 156-165.

Mitgang, Herbert. "Waiting for Beckett—And His *Happy Days* Premiere." *New York Times*, 17 September 1961, sec. 2, pp. 1, 3.

Modern Drama (December 1966). Special Beckett issue.

Montgomery, Niall. "No Symbols Where None Intended." *New World Writing*, V (April 1954), 324-337.

Moore, J. R. "Some Night Thoughts on Beckett." *Massachusetts Review*, VIII (Summer 1967), 529-539.

Moore, John. "A Farewell to Something." *Tulane Drama Review*, V (September 1960), 49-60.

Morrisette, B. "Les Idées de Robbe-Grillet sur Beckett." *La Revue des lettres modernes*, no. 100 (1964), pp. 55-68.

Morse, J. Mitchell. "The Choreography of the New Novel." *Hudson Review*, XVI (Autumn 1963), 396-419.

———. "Contemplative Life According to Samuel Beckett." *Hudson Review*, XV (Winter 1962-1963), 512-524.

———. "The Ideal Core of the Onion: Samuel Beckett's Criticism." *French Review*, XXXVIII (1964), 23-29.

Nadeau, Maurice. "Beckett: La Tragédie transposée en farce." *L'Avant-Scène*, no. 156 (1957), pp. 4-6.

———. "Le Chemin de la parole au silence." *Cahiers de la Compagnie Madeleine Renaud—Jean-Louis Barrault*, no. 44 (1963), pp. 63-66.

———. " 'La Dernière' tentative de Beckett." *Les Lettres Nouvelles*, I (September 1953), 860-864.

———. "Samuel Beckett, l'humour et le Néant." *Mercure de France*, CCCXII (August 1951), 693-697.

———. "Samuel Beckett ou le droit de silence." *Les Temps modernes*, no. 75 (January 1952), pp. 1273-1282.

Noon, William T. "God and Man in Twentieth Century Fiction." *Thought*, XXXVII (1962), 35-36.

———. "Modern Literature and the Sense of Time." *Thought*, XXXIII (Winter 1958-1959), 571-603.

Norès, Dominique. "La Condition humaine selon Beckett." *Théâtre d'Aujourd'hui*, no. 3 (September-October 1957), pp. 9-12.

Oates, J. C. "The Trilogy of Samuel Beckett." *Renascence*, XIV (Spring 1962), 160-165.

Oberg, Arthur K. *"Krapp's Last Tape* and the Proustian Vision." *Modern Drama*, IX (1966), 333-338.

O'Brien, Justin. "Samuel Beckett and André Gide: An Hypothesis." *French Review*, XL (1967), 485-486.

Olles, Helmut. "Samuel Beckett." *Welt und Wort*, xv (1960), 173-174.

O'Neill, Joseph P. "The Absurd in Samuel Beckett." *The Personalist*, xlviii (1967), 56-76.

Onimus, Jean. "L'Homme égaré: notes sur le sentiment d'égarement dans la littérature actuelle." *Etudes*, cclxxxiii (December 1954), 320-329.

Pallavicini, Roberto. "Aspetti della drammaturgia contemporanea." *Aut Aut*, nos. 79-80 (January-March 1964), pp. 68-73.

Paris, Jean. "The Clock Struck 29." *Reporter*, xv (4 October 1956), 39.

――――. "L'Engagement d'aujourd'hui." *Liberté*, iii (November 1961), 683-690.

Parker, R. B. "The Theory and Theatre of the Absurd." *Queen's Quarterly*, lxxiii (Autumn 1966), 421-441.

Paul, Leslie. "The Writer and the Human Condition." *Kenyon Review*, xxix (1967), 21-38.

Perniola, Mario. "Beckett e la scrittura esistenziale: Commento a *L'Innominabile*." *Tempo presente*, vi (1961), 727-733.

Perspective, xi (Autumn 1959). Special Beckett issue edited by Ruby Cohn.

Picchi, Mario. "Beckett: Malone muore." *La Fiera Letteraria*, 30 November 1958, p. 2.

――――. "Lettera romana: Conclusione su Beckett." *La Fiera Letteraria*, 4 January 1959, p. 6.

60

————. "Samuel Beckett—Introduzione." *La Fiera Letteraria*, 29 June 1958, p. 7.

Pingaud, Bernard. "*Molloy*." *Esprit*, IX (1951), 423-425.

————. "*Molloy* douze ans après." *Temps modernes*, XVIII (January 1963), 1283-1300.

Pinget, Robert. "*Old Tune*: Translated by Samuel Beckett." *New Yorker*, XXXVII (1 April 1961), 100.

Politzer, Heinz. "The Egghead Waits for Godot." *Christian Scholar*, VIII (March 1959), 46-50.

————. "From Nietzsche to Beckett: The Paradox of the Modern Parable." Paper read at the MLA Convention, 27 December 1959.

Popkin, Henry. "Williams, Osborne, or Beckett?" *New York Times Magazine*, 13 November 1960, pp. 32-33, 119-121.

Portal, Georges. "Pour l'amour de Dieu." *Ecrits de Paris*, nos. 195-196 (July-August 1961), pp. 139-146.

Pouillon, Jean. "*Molloy*." *Les Temps Modernes* (July 1951), pp. 184-186.

Pritchett, V. S. "Irish Oblomov." *New Statesman*, LIX (2 April 1960), 489.

Pronko, Leonard C. "Beckett, Ionesco, Schéadé: The Avant-Garde Theatre." *Modern Language Forum*, XLII (1958), 118-123.

Pullini, Giorgio et Renato Casarotto. "Da Patroni Griffi a Beckett a Venezia." *Letterature Moderne*, IX (May-June 1959), 366-376.

Radke, Judith Joy. "Doubt and Disintegration of Form in the French Novels and Dramas of Samuel Beckett. *Dissertation Abstracts*, XXII (1962), 3205-3206.

———. "Theater of Samuel Beckett: Une durée à animer." *Yale French Studies*, no. 29 (1962), pp. 57-64.

Raes, Hugo. "Samuel Beckett in Amerika." *Vlaamse Gids*, XLIII (July 1959), 495-496.

Rechtien, Brother John. "Time and Eternity Meet in the Present." *Texas Studies in Language and Literature*, VI (1964), 5-21.

Reid, Alec. "Beckett and the Drama of Unknowing." *Drama Survey*, II (Fall 1962), 130-138.

Rexroth, Kenneth. "The Point Is Irrelevance." *The Nation*, CLXXXII (14 April 1956), 325-328.

Rhodes, S. A. "From Godeau to Godot." *French Review*, XXXVI (January 1963), 260-265.

Rickels, Milton. "Existential Themes in Beckett's *Unnamable*." *Criticism*, IV (Spring 1962), 134-147.

Ricks, Christopher. "Beckett and the Lobster." *New Statesman*, LXVII (14 February 1964), 254-255.

———. "Congress Achieved." *New Statesman*, LXVII (17 April 1964), 604-605.

———. "The Roots of Samuel Beckett." *Listener*, LXXII (17 December 1964), 963-964, 980.

Rindauer, Gerhart. "Endspiel und neuer Anfang." *Forum* (Vienna), VIII (November 1961), 412-413.

Robbe-Grillet, Alain. "Samuel Beckett, auteur dramatique." *Critique*, IX (February 1953), 108-114.

Rosenberg, Marvin. "A Metaphor for Dramatic Form." *Journal of Aesthetics and Art Criticism*, XVII (December 1958), 174-180.

Rosi, Luca. "Beckett e il Teatro dell'assurdo." *Cenobio*, XIV (1965), 23-27.

Roy, Claude. "Samuel Beckett." *Nouvelle Revue française*, no. 143 (November 1964), pp. 885-890.

————. "L'Utilité de ne pas tout comprendre." *Nouvelle Revue française*, no. 124 (April 1963), pp. 703-709.

Rutherford, Malcolm. "Camp Tramps: *Waiting for Godot*." *Spectator*, CCXIV (8 January 1965), 42.

Sastre, Alfonso. "Siete notas sobre *Esperando a Godot*." *Primer Acto*, no. 1 (April 1957), pp. 46-52. Reprinted in *Casebook on Waiting for Godot*, edited by Ruby Cohn. New York: Grove Press, 1967, pp. 101-107.

Schechner, Richard. "Reality Is Not Enough; an Interview with A. Schneider." *Tulane Drama Review*, IX (Spring 1965), 118-152. Reply: E. Leontovich, X (Fall 1965), 214. Reprinted in *Casebook on Waiting for Godot*, edited by Ruby Cohn. New York: Grove Press, 1967, pp. 79-82.

————. "There's Lots of Time in *Godot*." *Modern Drama*, IX 1966), 268-276. Reprinted in *Casebook on Waiting for Godot*, edited by Ruby Cohn. New York: Grove Press, 1967, pp. 175-187.

Schneider, Alan. "Waiting for Beckett—A Personal Chronicle." *Chelsea Review*, no. 2 (Autumn 1958), pp. 3-20. Reprinted in *Casebook on Waiting for Godot*, edited by Ruby Cohn. New York: Grove Press, 1967, pp. 51-57.

Schneider, Pierre. "Play and Display." *The Listener*, LI (28 January 1954), 174-176.

Schumach, Murray. "Why They Wait for Godot." *New York Times Magazine*, 21 September 1958, pp. 36, 38, 41.

Scott, Nathan A., Jr. "The Recent Journey into the Zero Zone." *Centennial Review*, VI (Spring 1962), 144-181.

Schwarz, Karl. "Zeitproblematik in Samuel Becketts *En attendant Godot*." *Die Neueren Sprachen*, XVI (1967), 201-208.

Seaver, Richard. "Samuel Beckett." *Nimbus*, II (Autumn 1953), 61-62.

———. "Samuel Beckett: An Introduction." *Merlin*, I (Autumn 1952), 73-79.

Selz, Jean. "L'Homme finissant de Samuel Beckett." *Les Lettres nouvelles*, no. 51 (July-August 1957), pp. 120-123.

Senneff, Susan Field. "Song and Music in Samuel Beckett's *Watt*." *Modern Fiction Studies*, X (Summer 1964), 137-149.

Shartar, I. M. "The Theatre of the Mind: An Analysis of Works by Mallarmé, Yeats, Eliot, and Beckett." *Dissertation Abstracts*, XXVII (1967), 2161-A.

Sheedy, John J. "The Comic Apocalypse of King Hamm." *Modern Drama*, IX (1966), 310-318.

————. "The Net." In *Casebook on Waiting for Godot*, edited by Ruby Cohn. New York: Grove Press, 1967, pp. 159-166.

Shenker, Israel. "Moody Man of Letters." *New York Times*, 6 May 1956, sec. 2, p. 1.

Solomon, Philip H. "The Imagery of *Molloy* and Its Extension into Beckett's Other Fiction." *Dissertation Abstracts*, XXVIII (1968), 3198-A.

————. "Samuel Beckett's *Molloy*: A Dog's Life." *French Review*, XLI (1967), 84-91.

Steiner, George. "Books of Nuance and Scruple." *New Yorker*, XLIV (27 April 1968), 164, 167-170, 173-174.

Stottlar, James. "Samuel Beckett: An Introduction and an Interpretation." Master's thesis, Columbia University. 1957.

Strauss, Walter A. "Dante's Belacqua and Beckett's Tramps." *Comparative Literature*, XI (Summer 1959), 250-261.

Suvin, D. "Beckett's Purgatory of the Individual; or the Three Laws of Thermodynamics." *Tulane Drama Review*, XI (Summer 1967), 23-36. Reprinted in *Casebook on Waiting for Godot*, edited by Ruby Cohn. New York: Grove Press, 1967, pp. 121-132.

Tagliaferri, Aldo. "Il concreto e l'astratto in Beckett." *Verri*, no. 20 (1966), pp. 29-54.

Tallmer, Jerry. "The Magic Box." *Evergreen Review*, V (August 1961), 117-122.

Teyssèdre, Bernard. "Réalisme critique et avant-garde." *Les Lettres nouvelles*, no. 16 (July 1961), pp. 144-154.

Thibaudeau, Jean. "Un Théâtre de romanciers." *Critique*, nos. 159-160 (August-September 1960), pp. 686-692.

Thiebaut, Marcel. "Le 'Nouveau roman.' " *La Revue de Paris*, LXV (October 1958), 140-155.

Tindall, William York. "Beckett's Bums." *Critique*, II (Spring-Summer 1959), 3-15.

Todd, Robert E. "Proust and Redemption in *Waiting for Godot.*" *Modern Drama*, X (1967), 175-181.

Torrance, R. M. "Modes of Being and Time in the World of *Godot.*" *Modern Language Quarterly*, XXVIII (March 1967), 77-95.

Touchard, Pierre-Aimé. "Le Théâtre de Samuel Beckett." *La Revue de Paris*, LXVIII (February 1961), 73-87.

————. "Un Théâtre nouveau." *L'Avant-Scène*, no. 156 (1957), pp. 1-2.

Unterecker, John. "Samuel Beckett's No-Man's Land." *New Leader*, XLII (18 May 1959), 24-25.

Vahanian, Gabriel. "The Empty Cradle." *Theology Today*, 4 January 1957, pp. 521-526.

Verkein, Lea. "Samuel Beckett: een Classicus van de Aventgarde?" *Vlaamse Gids*, XLV (January 1961), 62-63.

————. "Wachten met Beckett." *Vlaamse Gids*, XLIII (December 1959), 842-845.

Via, D. O., Jr. "*Waiting for Godot* and Man's Search for Community." *Journal of Bible and Religion* (January 1962), pp. 32-37.

Viatte, Auguste. "La Littérature dans l'impasse." *La Revue de l'Université Laval*, XV (November 1960), 254-259.

――――. "Le 'Nouveau roman.' " *La Revue de l'Université Laval*, XVI (*October* 1961), 122-128.

Vigée, Claude. "Les Artistes de la faim." *Comparative Literature*, IX (Spring 1957), 97-117.

Vold, Jan Erik. "Samuel Becketts romaner." *Samtiden*, LXXIV (1965), 441-447.

Walker, Roy. "Love, Chess, and Death: Samuel Beckett's Double Bill." *Twentieth Century*, CLXIV (December 1958), 532-540.

――――. "Shagreen Shamrock." *The Listener*, LVII (24 January 1957), 167-168.

Warhaft, Sidney. "Threne and Theme in *Watt*." *Wisconsin Studies in Contemporary Literature*, IV (1963), 261-278.

Weales, Gerald. "The Language of *Endgame*." *Tulane Drama Review*, VI (June 1962), 107-117.

Webb, E., III. "Samuel Beckett, Novelist: A Study of His Trilogy." *Dissertation Abstracts*, XXVIII (1968), 4191-A.

Wellershoff, Dieter. "Gescheiterte Enthymthologisierung: Zu den Romanen Samuel Becketts." *Merkur*, XVII (1963), 528-546.

Wellwarth, G. E. "Life in the Void: Samuel Beckett." *University of Kansas City Review*, XXVIII (October 1961), 25-33.

Welsbacher, Richard Charles. "Four Projections of Absurd Existence." *Dissertation Abstracts*, xxv (1965), 7423-7424.

Wendler, Herbert W. "Graveyard Humanism." *Southwestern Review*, xlix (Winter 1964), 44-52.

Wilcock, J. Rodolfo. "Nulla da fare." *Il Mondo*, 17 October 1961, p. 14.

Wilson, Colin. "Existential Criticism." *Chicago Review*, xiii (Summer 1959), 152-181.

Wilson, R. N. "Samuel Beckett: The Social Psychology of Emptiness." *Journal of Social Issues*, xx (January 1964), 62-70.

Worms, Jeannine. "Poésie et Roman—compassion et beauté." *Mercure de France*, no. 1180 (December 1961), pp. 650-656.

Worsley, T. C. "Cactus Land." *New Statesman and Nation*, 13 August 1955, pp. 184-185.

Worth, Katherine J. "Yeats and the French Drama." *Modern Drama*, viii (1966), 382-391.

Yerles, Pierre. "Le Théâtre de Samuel Beckett." *Revue Nouvelle*, xxxiii (April 1961), 401-406.

Zeraffa, Michael. "Le Théâtre—Beckett, Schehadé, Shakespeare." *Europe*, xxxv (December 1957), 159-162.

Unsigned. "The Anti-Novel in France." *Times Literary Supplement* (London), 13 February 1959, p. 82.

———. "Beckett." *New Yorker*, xl (8 August 1964), 22-23.

————. "Beckett and the Theatre of the Concrete." *Time*, LXXXI (28 June 1963), 48-50.

————. [Beckett as a Dramatist]. *New York Times*, 24 September 1967, sec. 2, p. 1.

————. "Beckett plus Brecht." *Dialog*, XI (1966), 129-132.

————. [*Cascando*]. *The Times* (London), 7 October 1964, p. 8.

————. [Comment on Film of Beckett's *Play*]. *New York Times*, 27 February 1966, sec. 2, p. 13.

————. "Comment—*Waiting for Godot*." *Meanjin*, IV (Winter 1956), 132.

————. "Dublin Honorary Degrees." *The Times* (London). 26 February 1959, p. 12.

————. "*Eh, Joe: Plans*." *The Times* (London), 26 November 1965, p. 15.

————. "*Embers: Award*." *The Times* (London), 15 September 1959, p. 5.

————. [*Endgame*]. *The Times* (London), 7 November 1963, p. 16.

————. [*Endgame*]. *The Times* (London), 10 July 1964, p. 7.

————. [*Endgame*: plans]. *The Times* (London), 18 September 1961, p. 14.

————. "Entertainment from the Works of End of the Day." *The Times* (London), 18 October 1962, p. 18.

———. "Foreign Origins." *Times Literary Supplement* (London), 27 May 1955, p. x.

———. "Happy Days." *The Times* (London), 17 November 1961, p. 21.

———. "Happy Days." *The Times* (London), 2 November 1962, p. 6.

———. [Honorary Degree]. *The Times* (London), 3 July 1959, p. 9.

———. "Life in the Mud." *Times Literary Supplement*, 7 April 1961, p. 168.

———. "Long Wait." *Times Literary Supplement* (London), 5 May 1961, p. 277.

———. [May Produce the First Play at Oxford Theatre in Memory]. *The Times*, (London), 15 November 1967, p. 10.

———. "Messenger of Gloom." *The Observer* (London), 9 November 1958.

———. "Novels of 1964: Samuel Beckett." *Times Literary Supplement*, III, pp. 45-47. [About *How It Is.*]

———. "*The Old Tune.*" *The Times* (London), 24 November 1964, p. 15.

———. "Oxford Experimental Theatre to be Named after Him." *The Times* (London), 17 October 1967, p. 9.

———. "Paradise of Indignity." *Times Literary Supplement* (London), 28 March 1958, p. 168.

————. "Plans to Write Film Episode." *The Times* (London), 13 November 1963, p. 5.

————. *"Play."* *The Times* (London), 8 April 1964, p. 10.

————. "Problems That Confront the New Abbey Theatre." *Irish Digest*, LXXVIII (October 1963), 79-82.

————. "Puzzling about *Godot.*" *Times Literary Supplement* (London), 13 April 1956, p. 221.

————. "Samuel Beckett: Une thèse, un livre." *Caliban*, N.S., I (1965), 159-166.

————. [Signatory to Declaration against Performances of Plays in South African Theatres with Color Bar]. *The Times* (London), 26 June 1963, p. 12.

————. "10s for the Film Rights of *Act Without Words.*" *The Times* (London), 25 April 1966, p. 16.

————. "To Stage Own Play at W. Berlin Arts Festival." *The Times* (London), 17 August 1967, p. 6.

————. "The Train Stops." *Times Literary Supplement* (London), 6 September 1957, p. 604.

————. *"The Unnamable: Plans."* *The Times* (London), 8 January 1959, p. 5.

————. *"Oh les beaux jours."* *New Yorker*, XL (22 February 1964), 102-104.

————. [U.S. Performance of *Happy Days*]. *The Times* (London), 19 September 1961, p. 14.

————. *"Waiting for Godot." The Times* (London), 4 September 1962, p. 7 [Also comment on *Actes sans paroles*: film plans.]

————. *"Waiting for Godot." The Times* (London), 31 December 1964, p. 4.

————. *"Waiting for Godot." The Times* (London), 16 January 1965, p. 5.

————. "Why Actors Are Fascinated by Beckett's Theatre." *The Times* (London), 27 February 1965, p. 14.

————. "Why Samuel Beckett Writes in French." *Books Abroad*, XXIII (Summer 1949), 247-248.

————. *"Words and Music*: BBC Performance Plans." *The Times* (London), 1 November 1962, p. 8.

E. Reviews of Beckett's Books
A Selected Checklist

Acts Without Words

Unsigned. *The Times* (London), 12 January 1966, p. 13.

————. *Spectator*, CCIX (27 July 1962), 115.

————. *The Times* (London), 26 January 1960, p. 12.

————. *The Times* (London), 3 July 1962, p. 15.

————. *The Times* (London), 24 January 1966, p. 14.

All That Fall

Fay, Gerald. *Manchester Guardian*, 15 October 1957, p. 6.

Freedley, George. *Library Journal*, LXXXII (15 December 1957), 3214.

Logue, Chistopher. *New Statesman*, LIV (14 September 1957), 325.

Strachey, Julia. *Spectator*, CXCIX (20 September 1957), 373.

Unsigned. *Times Literary Supplement* (London), 6 September 1957, 528.

Anthology of Mexican Poetry
Ulibarri, Sabine R. *New Mexico Quarterly*, XXIX
(1959), 355-356.

————. *Times Literary Supplement* (London),
6 February 1959, p. 72.

Come and Go
Hodgart, M. *Manchester Guardian*, 27 July 1967, 11.

Ricks, Christopher. *Listener*, LXXVIII (3 August 1967), 148.

Wilson, A. *Observer* (London), 16 July 1967, p. 20.

Comment c'est [How It Is]
Baro, Gene. *New York Times Book Review*, 22 March
1964, p. 5.

Cruttwell, Patrick. *Hudson Review*, (Summer 1964), p. 303.

Federman, Raymond. *Books Abroad*, (Autumn 1961), p. 337.

————. *French Review*, (May 1961), p. 594.

Fletcher, John. *Lettres nouvelles*, XIII (April 1961), 169-171.

Furbank, P. N. *New York Times*, June 1964, p. 69.

Glauber, R. H. *Christian Century*, LXXXI (8 April 1964), 461.

Johnson, B. S. *Spectator*, CCXII (26 June 1964), 850.

Jost, E. F. *America*, CX (29 February 1964), 291.

Kermode, Frank. *New York Review of Books*, II
(19 March 1964), 9.

Luccioni, G. *Esprit* (April 1961), pp. 710-713.

Nadeau, Maurice. *L'Express*, 26 January 1961, pp. 25-26.

Piatier, Jacqueline. *Le monde*, 11 February 1961, p. 9.

Pritchett, V. S. *New Statesman*, LXVII (1 May 1964), 683.

Pryce-Jones, A. *New York Herald Tribune*, 29 February 1964, p. 13.

Simon, John. *Bookweek*, 8 March 1964, p. 5.

Sutherland, D. *The New Leader*, 11 May 1964, p. 12.

Updike, John. *New Yorker*, XL (19 December 1964), 165.

Unsigned. *New Mexico Quarterly Review*, XXXIV (Spring 1964), 116-17.

——. *Newsweek* (24 February 1964), p. 93.

——. *Time* (28 February 1964), p. 108.

——. *Times Literary Supplement* (London), 7 April 1961, p. 213.

——. *Times Literary Supplement* (London), 21 May 1964, p. 429.

——. *New York Times Book Review*, 22 March 1964, p. 5.

——. *The Times* (London), 7 May 1964, p. 18.

La Dernière Bande

Unsigned. *Times Literary Supplement* (London), 28 April 1961, p. 262.

Eh Joe and Other Writings

Hodgart, M. *Manchester Guardian*, 27 July 1967, 11.

Johnson, B. S. *New Statesman*, LXXIV (14 July 1967), 54.

Ricks, Christopher. *Listener*, LXXVIII (3 August 1967), 148.

Wilson, A. *Observer* (London), 16 July 1967, p. 20.

Embers

Federman, Raymond. *Books Abroad* (Autumn 1960), p. 361.

Unsigned. *The Times* (London), 25 June 1959, p. 5.

Endgame

Driver, Tom F. *Christian Century*, LXXV (5 March 1958),
    282-283.

Hatch, Robert. *Nation*, CLXXXVI (15 February 1958), 145-146.

Hewes, Henry. *Saturday Review*, XLI (15 February 1958), 28.

————. *New Statesman*, LVI (8 November 1958), 630.

————. *Spectator*, CCI (7 November 1958), 609.

————. *Accent*, XX (Autumn 1960), 223-234.

————. *Illustrated London News*, CCXXX (20 April 1957), 652.

Unsigned. *Life*, XLII (22 April 1957), 143.

————. *Theatre Arts*, XLII (April 1958), 26.

————. *Newsweek*, LIX (26 February 1962), 79.

From An Abandoned Work
Mayoux, Jean-Jacques. *Etudes anglaises*, XII (1959), 181-182.

Happy Days
Brustein, Robert. *New Republic* (2 October 1961), pp. 45-46.

Clurman, Harold. *Nation* (7 October 1961), pp. 234-235.

————. *Nation* (18 October 1965), pp. 258-259.

Driver, Tom F. "Unsweet Song," *Christian Century* (11 October 1961), pp. 1208-1209.

Garcoigne, Bamber. *Spectator*, CCIX (9 November 1962), 715-717.

Gilman, Richard. *Commonwealth* (13 October 1961), pp. 69-70.

Hewes, Henry. *Saturday Review* (7 October 1961), p. 38.

Johnson, Bryan S. *Spectator*, CCIX (20 July 1962), 92.

McAleer, John J. *Books Abroad* (Winter 1963), p. 79.

Unsigned. *Drama*, no. 68 (Spring 1963), p. 20.

————. *Educational Theatre Journal*, XII (December 1961), 293-294.

————. *Hudson Review*, XIV (Winter 1961-1962), 589.

————. *New Statesman* (9 November 1962), p. 679.

————. *New Yorker*, XXXVII (30 September 1961), 119.

————. *Spectator*, CCIX (9 November 1962), 715.

———. *Theatre Arts* (8 November 1961), pp. 57-58.

———. *Time* (29 September 1961), p. 74.

———. *Times Literary Supplement* (London), 21 December 1962, p. 988.

Imagination Dead Imagine
O'Hara, J. D. *Carleton Miscellany*, VIII (Winter 1967), 108.

Taubman, R. *New Statesman*, LXXI (18 February 1966), 232.

Unsigned. *Times Literary Supplement* (London), 30 June 1966, p. 570.

Krapp's Last Tape
Brustein, Robert. *New Republic*, CXLII (22 February 1960), 21.

Clurman, Harold. *Nation*, CXC (13 February 1960), 153.

Driver, Tom F. *Christian Century*, LXXVII (2 March 1960), 256-257.

Federman, Raymond. *Books Abroad* (Autumn 1960), p. 361.

Hewes, Henry. *Saturday Review*, XLIII (30 January 1960), 28.

Unsigned. *New Yorker*, XXXV (23 January 1960), 75.

———. *Spectator*, CCI (7 November 1958), 609.

More Pricks Than Kicks
Muir, Edwin. *The Listener*, XLI (4 July 1934), 42.

Murphy

Cahoon, Herbert. *Library Journal*, LXXXII (1 April 1957), 985.

Fiedler, Leslie. *New York Times Book Review*, 14 April 1957, p. 27.

Greene, Henry. *Chicago Sunday Tribune*, 28 April 1957, p. 7.

Johnson, B. S. *Spectator*, CCXI (13 December 1963), 800.

Mercier, Vivian. *Commonweal*, LXVI (17 May 1957), 188-190.

Powell, D. *Sunday Times*, 13 March 1938, p. 8.

Ross, M. *The Listener*, LXXI (23 January 1964), 165.

Tracy, Honor. *New Republic*, CXXXVI (6 May 1957), 19.

Unsigned. *Time*, LXIX (18 March 1957), 108.

————. *Times Literary Supplement* (London), 12 March 1938, p. 172.

————. *Times Literary Supplement* (London), 30 January 1964, p. 81.

No's Knife

Burgess, A. *Spectator*, CCXIX (21 July 1967), 79.

Hodgart, M. *Manchester Guardian*, XCVII (27 July 1967), 11.

Johnson, B. S. *New Statesman*, LXXIV (14 July 1967), 54.

Kingston, J. *Punch*, CCLIII (2 August 1967), 182.

Ricks, Christopher. *The Listener*, LXXVIII (3 August 1967), 148.

Wilson, A. *Observer* (London), 16 July 1967, p. 20.

The Old Tune

Unsigned. *The Times* (London), 25 August 1960, p. 12.

Play

Brustein, Robert. *New Republic*, CL (1 February 1964), 30.

Calder, John. *Times Literary Supplement* (London),
23 April 1964, p. 343.

Clurman, Harold. *Nation*, CXCVIII (27 January 1964), 106-107.

Gavin, Ewart. *London Magazine* (May 1964), p. 95.

Gilman, Richard. *Commonwealth*, LXXIX (24 January
1964), 484-485.

Hewes, Henry. *Saturday Review*, XLVII (25 January 1964), 25.

Johnson, B. S. *Spectator*, CCXII (26 June 1964), 858.

Pokin, Henry. *Vogue*, CXLIII (15 February 1964), 22.

Walker, Roy. *Times Literary Supplement* (London),
16 April 1964, p. 311.

Unsigned. *Time*, LXXXIII (17 January 1964), 64.

———. *The Times* (London), 24 June 1963, p. 14.

———. *Times Literary Supplement* (London),
9 April 1964, p. 292.

Poems in English

Davie, Donald. *New Statesman*, LXIII (5 January 1962), 20.

Burke, Herbert. *Library Journal*, 1 June 1963, p. 2257.

Furbank, P. N. *New Statesman*, LXIII (8 February 1962), 265.

Griffin, L. W. *Library Journal*, LXXXIX (1 May 1964), 1964.

Merritt, J. D. *Books Abroad* (Spring 1964), p. 192.

Stephanchev, Stephen. *New York Herald Tribune Book Review*, 11 August 1963, p. 6.

Unsigned. *Times Literary Supplement* (London), 25 May 1962, p. 234.

Proust

Donoghue, D. *New Statesman*, LXXI (25 March 1966), 428.

Unsigned. *Times Literary Supplement* (London), 30 December 1965, p. 1208.

Stories and Texts for Nothing
[*Nouvelles et Textes pour rien*]

Curley, Dorothy. *Library Journal*, XCII (July 1967), 2600.

Davis, D. M. *National Observer*, VI (25 September 1967), 25.

Hayes, Richard. *Commonweal*, LXIV (24 May 1956), 203.

Hodgart, Matthew. *New York Review of Books*, IX (7 December 1967), 3.

Maddocks, Melvin. *Christian Science Monitor*, 27 July 1967, p. 7.

Maloff, Saul. *Newsweek*, LXX (4 September 1967), 75E.

Muggeridge, M. *Esquire*, LXVIII (September 1967), 14.

Poore, C. *New York Times*, CXVI (20 July 1967), 39M.

Rotondaro, F. *Best Sellers*, XXVII (1 August 1967), 166.

Unsigned. *Booklist and Subscription Books Bulletin*, LXIV (15 November 1967), 375.

――――. *Kirkus Service*, XXXV (1 June 1967), 658.

――――. *New York Times Book Review*, 12 November 1967, p. 67.

――――. *Publisher's Weekly*, CLXLI (5 June 1967), 169.

――――. *Time*, XC (14 July 1967), 90.

Trilogy: *Molloy, Malone Dies, and The Unnamable*
[This section includes reviews of the individual novels as well as those which deal with the entire trilogy.]

Barrett, William. *New York Times Book Review*, 16 September 1956, p. 5.

Breit, H. *New York Times Book Review*, 11 April 1954, p. 8.

Coleman, John. *Spectator*, CCIV (8 April 1960), 516.

Duchene, Anne. *Manchester Guardian*, 14 April 1960, p. 10.

Finn, James. *Commonweal*, LXV (7 December 1956), 257.

Fouchet, M. P. *Carrefour* (24 April 1951), p. 8.

Fowlie, Wallace. *New York Herald Tribune Book Review*, 23 November 1958, p. 4.

Heppenstall, R. *Observer* (London), 10 March 1960.

Hicks, Granville. *Saturday Review*, XLI (4 October 1958), 14.

Hodgart, Patricia. *Manchester Guardian*, 21 September 1956, p. 6.

Kanters, R. *L'Age Nouveau*, (June 1951).

Mercier, Vivian. *Nation*, CLXXXVIII (14 February 1959), 144.

Mills, R. J. *Christian Century*, LXXVI (30 December 1959), 1524.

Paulding, Gouverneur. *New York Herald Tribune Book Review*, 16 September 1956, p. 2.

Pingaud, Bernard. *Esprit*, IX (1951), 423-425.

Pouillon, Jean. *Les Temps modernes*, LXIX (July 1951), 184-186.

Pritchett, V. S. *New Statesman*, LIX (2 April 1960), 489.

Stone, Jerome. *Saturday Review*, XXXIX (27 October 1956), 25.

Spender, Stephen. *New York Times Book Review*, 12 October 1958, p. 5.

Zinnes, Harriet. *Books Abroad*, (Autumn 1960), p. 401.

Unsigned. *Punch*, CCLI (19 October 1966), 605.

———. *Saturday Review*, XLVIII (31 July 1965), 26.

———. *Books and Bookman*, XII (February 1967), 57.

———. *Time*, 15 October 1956, p. 118.

———. *Times Literary Supplement* (London), 17 June 1960, p. 381.

———. *Time*, 13 October 1958, p. 107.

Waiting for Godot

Anouilh, Jean. *Arts*, no. 400 (27 January 1953).

Audiberti, Jacques. *Arts*, no. 394 (16 January 1953).

Fraser, G. S. *Times Literary Supplement* (London), 10 February 1956, p. 84.

Freedley, George. *Library Journal*, LXXIX (15 December 1954), 2460.

Gibbs, Wokott. *New Yorker*, XXXII (5 May 1956), 89.

Hewes, Henry. *Saturday Review*, XL (9 February 1957), 25.

Hobson, Harold. *The Sunday Times* (London), 7 August 1955.

Johnston, Denis. *Irish Writing*, no. 34 (Spring 1956), pp. 23-28.

Kennebeck, Edwin. *Commonweal*, LXI (31 December 1954), 365-366.

Mannes, Marya. *The Reporter* (20 October 1955).

Salacrou, Armand. *Arts*, no. 400 (27 January 1953).

Williams, R. *New Statesman*, LXI (19 May 1961), 802.

Zegel, Sylvain. *La Libération*, 7 January 1953.

Unsigned. *Time*, LXIX (18 March 1957), 108.

———. *English*, XI (Spring 1956), 18.

———. *New York Times Magazine*, 21 September 1958, p. 36.

———. *San Quentin News*, XVIII (28 November 1957).

———. *Theatre Arts*, XLI (April 1957), 16.

———. *Theology Today*, XIII (January 1957), 521-526.

———. *The Times* (London), 28 April 1960, p. 6.

———. *Times Literary Supplement* (London), 10 February 1956, p. 84.

———. *Illustrated London News*, CCXXVII (1 October 1955), 582.

———. *New Statesman*, L (13 August 1955), 184.

———. *Spectator*, CXCV (12 August 1955), 222.

Watt

Abbey, Edward. *New Mexico Quarterly*, XXIX (1959), 381-383.

Atkinson, Brooks. *Venture*, III (1959), 69-70.

Baro, Gene. *New York Herald Book Review*, 5 July 1959, p. 6.

Barr, Donald. *New York Times Book Review*, 21 June 1959, p. 4.

Johnson, B. S. *Spectator*, CCXI (13 December 1963), 800.

Mauroc, Daniel. *Table Ronde*, (October 1953), pp. 155-156.

Mercier, Vivian. *Nation*, CLXXXVIII (February 1959), 144-145.

Ross, M. *The Listener*, LXXI (23 January 1964), 165.

Unsigned. *New York Times Book Review*, 21 June 1959, p. 4.

———. *Time*, LXXIII (1 June 1959), 90.

———. *Times Literary Supplement* (London), 30 January 1964, p. 8.